2018 Edition

Buying a Home in Texas

Don't Let Them Make a Monkey Out of You!

Alysse Musgrave

Alysse Musgrave/
Dallas, Houston, Austin
www.HelpUBuyAmerica.com

This publication is designed to provide accurate and authoritative information with regard to the subject matter covered. It is sold with the understanding that the author and the publisher are not engaged in rendering legal, intellectual property, accounting, or other professional advice.

The author and publisher, individually or corporately, do not accept any responsibility for any liabilities resulting from the actions of any parties involved.

Buying a Home in Texas: Don't Let Them Make a Monkey Out of You!/ Alysse Musgrave. – 3rd ed.
ISBN-13: 978-1983978432 ISBN-10: 1983978434

To my beautiful daughter, Lia, who really, really hates it when I mention her in my books. Mommy loves you, Punkin'.

If you can't explain it simply, you don't understand it well enough.

—ALBERT EINSTEIN

Table of Contents

Introduction

Let's face it. In a real estate transaction, the buyer assumes all of the risk. The seller walks away from the property and is free of any obligation or responsibility. The buyer pays for inspections, appraisals, closing costs, and ends up with the house and a mortgage. At best, buying a home is a complicated process. At worst, it can be an emotional and financial nightmare. Not only do you have to find a house that you love, you have to verify its condition, negotiate a good price, figure out how to pay for it, insure it, move in, all the while ensuring you are buying a home that you will be able to resell for a profit when the time comes. The list of things to consider is seemingly endless.

Before 1989, all real estate agents worked for the seller. The agent would spend many days in the car with a potential buyer, and that buyer had no idea that the agent had a fiduciary duty to tell the seller everything the buyer said. If the buyer offered $400,000 for a house but stated that they would be willing to go up to $450,000, for example, the agent was required *by law* to pass that information along to the seller. The law of the land was "caveat emptor," let the buyer beware.

As expected, lawsuits were filed across the country when buyers learned that they could have purchased the property for a lot less money had they known whom the agent represented. As a result, most states implemented disclosure requirements. At the first *substantive* meeting with a potential buyer or seller, agents were required to disclose which party they represented. Most states implemented additional policies and procedures that gave the *illusion* of fairness, but one thing remained the same: The buyer still assumes the risk and the buyer is still the target of most of the fraud.

Exclusive Buyer Agency was born in 1989, finally providing the buyer with the opportunity to buy a home with the same level of representation that sellers have always enjoyed. But, since there are relatively few agents who work with buyers exclusively, most buyers are forced to accept substandard representation.

The real estate system in this country is broken and there is no easy fix. In a perfect world, each party to the transaction would pay for their own representation. Commissions would be fixed since it's no more work to help someone buy a $600,000 house than it is to help them buy a $100,000 house. Buyers, however, don't want to pay their own agent because they need cash for their down payment and closing costs. Real estate brokerages aren't going to cut profits and change tried and true business models voluntarily, so herein lies the issue. Buyers have to learn to navigate through a homebuying process in which mortgage fraud runs rampant and where buyers very rarely have proper representation.

My goal in writing this book is not to teach you everything there is to know about buying a home; there are thousands of variables. My goal is to share information that will help you make good choices and will help you recognize fraud when they see it.

So who am I? My name is Alysse Musgrave, and I am the broker and owner of one of the oldest and most successful exclusive buyer brokerages in Texas. Since 1995, I have been protecting the rights of homebuyers, speaking out against predatory lending practices, and have saved my clients thousands and thousands of dollars. I am one of a relatively few number of exclusive buyer brokers in this country, and we're all committed to the same cause: to keep homebuyers from getting ripped off.

In the pages that follow, I'll share with you all the information I share with my own clients, and hopefully my words and advice will lead to a seamless and stress-free homebuying experience and years of comfort and financial happiness in your new home.

About This Book

It's been said that a good non-fiction book conveys to the reader only the necessary information – and not one word more.

That's what I do in this book. I tell you only what you really need to know, and I leave out all the fluff. You'll notice that I didn't include links to mortgage calculators or to the HUD website. There isn't a glossary with the definitions of a thousand words you really don't need to know.

In this book, I strive to teach you things that no other Realtor will tell you. You will learn how to recognize a good floor plan, how to negotiate with the seller, how to get the information you really need from your loan officer, and much more.

Since the first publication of this book, I've answered *hundreds* of emails from homebuyers who had questions about the buying process or who needed a referral to a buyer-friendly agent in their area. As a thank you for buying this book, I'd like to welcome you to contact me anytime at Alysse@HelpUBuyAmerica.com with any questions you may have and to tell me about your homebuying experience. I hope it will be a good one.

{ 1 }

Real Estate Agents

A real estate agent is a person who is licensed to list and sell real estate; a Realtor is a real estate agent who is also a member of the National Association of Realtors. A Realtor is always a real estate agent, but not every real estate agent is a Realtor. In this book, I use the terms "agent" and "Realtor" interchangeably.

People have come to assume that Realtors have no value, especially since the database of homes for sale known as the Multiple Listing Service (MLS) has become accessible to anyone with a computer and online access. It doesn't help that Realtors in general rank just below car salesmen in likeability and trustworthiness. However, the truth is that a *good* real estate agent can save you tens of thousands of dollars and substantially reduce the risks involved with purchasing a home. A bad one can do the opposite, and you'll probably be none the wiser.

Searching the MLS for a home is something you can do on your own. To get inside the house you need an agent. But any monkey can open the door to a house! That's not where the value of a Realtor lies.

A Realtor's value lies in his or her knowledge of pricing, market-ing, marketability, finance, hazard insurance, title insurance, surveys, and in their ability to negotiate a great price and protect your rights as a homebuyer.

Most agents will tell you that it took 7-10 transactions before they felt 100% comfortable with the process. To think you can buy a home without an agent simply because you read "Homebuying for Dummies" or this book is a mistake. You need an agent or a lawyer; sometimes you need both.

When hiring an agent, it is important that you find a highly trained career agent. It benefits you to work with a Realtor who makes his or her living working in real estate or is transitioning to do so. Your cousin's mother-in-law who sells one or two homes a year may not be qualified to protect you. You want a well-respected, experienced Realtor. Next, you need the right type of representation. The following types of agents are the agents with which you should be familiar: exclusive buyer agents, buyer agents, dual agents, seller agents, real estate consultants, and discounters. In the following sections, I will describe the roles of these agents.

Exclusive Buyer Agents

An Exclusive Buyer Agent (EBA) works in an office that never takes listings and never represents sellers. It's all buyers, all the time. There is absolutely no conflict of interest that could jeopardize your negotiating position. To understand the importance of hiring an Exclusive Buyer Agent, you need to learn about *fiduciary duty.*

A fiduciary duty is a legal duty to act solely in another party's interest. It's the same duty that an attorney owes his or her client. When you work with an EBA, they have a legal, fiduciary duty to negotiate on *your* behalf. Their goal is to help you buy the home of your choice at the *lowest* possible price and with the best terms. By law, they will owe you the following:

- Loyalty
- Complete confidentiality
- Obedience
- Full disclosure
- Complete accounting for all funds
- Fairness and honesty

Only a single agent (vs. a dual agent) can be fiduciary. You can't have a fiduciary duty to a buyer and a seller at the same time.

> *If the agent you hire to represent you works in a traditional real estate office that takes listings and represents sellers, they are not and cannot be an Exclusive Buyer Agent.*

All the financial good guys like Dave Ramsey, Ralph Nadar, Suze Orman, and Jane Chatzky advocate for Exclusive Buyer Agencies.

> *Hiring an EBA is the single most important thing you can do to protect yourself when you're buying a home.*

Here's the bad news. Less than ½ of 1% of Realtors across the country work as Exclusive Buyer Agents, and it can be difficult – if not impossible – to find an EBA in some areas. Why? EBAs earn half of what a dual agent earns in any given transaction, so it can be difficult to convince a real estate agent to work only with buyers. It's easier to take a listing, put a sign in the yard, and to wait for an uneducated buyer to come along. My company currently serves homebuyers in Dallas, Austin, and Houston. If you're searching for an EBA outside of these areas, you can send an email to Help@HelpUBuyAmerica.com and we'll help you find someone.

Buyer Agents

Buyer agents work for traditional real estate companies that represent both buyers and sellers (Re/Max, Keller Williams, Ebby Halliday, Century

21, etc.). There are incentives and pressure for these agents to try to sell in-house listings, so they essentially are not working for the buyer, even if they claim otherwise. If your traditional buyer agent shows you a home listed by someone in their office and you decide you want to buy it, the office has procedures to "represent" both sides of the transaction. These types of offices tend to favor the seller more than the buyer, as evidenced by all the ads telling you how much they have "sold." As a buyer, you are not looking to be "sold," you want to "save" and not get ripped off!

Dual Agents/Intermediaries

A dual agent is one that works for the buyer and the seller in the same transaction. It's comparable to a lawyer representing both the husband and the wife in a divorce.

A servant cannot serve two masters! It's simply impossible.

Dual agency is illegal in nearly every other industry, but somehow it continues to exist in the world of real estate. In my view, and in the eyes of most consumer advocates, it's a form of fraud.

Technically, dual agency is not legal in Texas, but there is always a way around the law that works against both sellers and buyers, and it's still quite difficult to tell the difference between a "buyer agent" and a "dual agent," or a "seller agent" and a "dual agent." Should a Texas Realtor, for example, wish to sell a seller/client's house to one of their buyer/clients, they use a third party *in their office* to handle negotiations for one of the parties. This party is called an intermediary. The intermediary's job is to negotiate the price and terms of the real estate transaction *without giving advice to either party.* Sellers are paying a real estate broker thousands of dollars to sell their home, but their agent won't help them get a higher sales price. Buyers are on their own with respect to pricing, property condition, and negotiations. The intermediary can, for example, give the buyer a list of homes that have sold in the neighborhood, but they can't suggest a fair sales price. They can give them a list of home inspectors, but they won't warn them to walk away from a property due to its condition. The Realtors become order takers, and the buyer and seller foot the bill.

The following scenario illustrates what it's like to work with a dual agent or intermediary. Suppose you drive by a house that interests you and notice that there is a Best Realty sign in the yard. You decide to call the number printed on the sign, and a very nice Realtor answers the call.

This Realtor was hired by the owners of the house to sell their property and to negotiate the highest price on their behalf.

On the phone, the Realtor offers to show you the house, so you set up a time to meet and view her listing. You like the house but are not ready to commit, so the Realtor offers to show you some other homes that you might like.

While looking at the first house, the Realtor represented the seller. Now they are showing you other agent's listings in which they would represent you as a buyer agent, should you opt to buy one of those houses.

In the meantime, they've asked you all kinds of questions and have a clear picture of your purchasing power and your level of motivation. If you decide to buy the first house they showed you (or any of their other listings), they'd have to turn you over to someone else in their office, the intermediary, but would still be legally obligated to tell their seller/client everything they know about you. And, from the seller's standpoint, the agent used their house as a source of buyer leads. The seller most likely shared all of their secrets with this agent, only to have that information used against them if both the buyer side and seller side of the transaction are handled in-house with the same broker. It's a convoluted mess, and it is unfair to both the seller and the buyer; the only person who wins here is the dual agent Realtor and their broker.

Seller Agents

Seller agents work in a traditional real estate office that takes listings or represent sellers. They become dual agents when they represent the buyer. I have yet to meet an agent who only represents sellers; double dipping by representing both sellers and buyers is very, very lucrative (as are most forms of fraud).

Real Estate Consultant/Fee for Services

Real estate consultants typically offer services to buyers and sellers on an a la carte basis. For example, instead of paying a six percent commission, a seller can pay a consultant a fixed rate to list the home on the MLS or to provide a market analysis. Buyers can pay an agent a fee just to write the purchase contract or to show them a specific home. This is a great way, in my opinion, for real estate to be bought and sold, and more Realtors are beginning to offer these services. These services are, however, more beneficial for the seller than for the buyer.

Discounters

Most Realtors detest the idea of discounting their commission; I don't. I think if a buyer can do much of the legwork, they are entitled to part of the commission.

> *Most discounters are rebating commissions because they can't compete with other agents in their area; they can only compete on price.*

Or, they are online-only brokers that you never meet, and they never see the house you are buying; they only serve to write the contracts and manage the transaction. *My advice is to stay away from these types.* If you can find a busy career agent who will reduce his or her commission by offering a reduced level of service, but will still offer you advice and guidance, it can be a great way to buy a house.

A really good agent, however, is not going to do the same amount of work for less money. Would you?

How Agents Get Paid

Real estate commissions are generally a seller's expense (which is why the industry is seller driven). When a homeowner decides to sell their home, they typically hire a traditional Realtor who works with both buyers and sellers. Commissions are negotiable, but are typically 5-7 percent of the sale price. The Realtor lists the home on the MLS and, by doing so, agrees to split the commission with the agent who brings a qualified buyer. At closing, the seller's proceeds are reduced in the amount of the negotiated commission. That amount is split between the buyer broker and the listing broker. Agents work under a broker and get paid out of their broker's share of the commission.

To illustrate, let's assume an agent takes a listing on a $200,000 house, and the seller agrees to pay the broker a 6% commission. The house sells for the list price, and the listing broker and the buyer agent's broker each get half of the commission, or $6,000 each ($200,000 sales price x 0.06 commission ÷ 2). The broker shares most of that $6,000 with their agent.

Some buyers believe that they can get a better price for a home if no Realtor is involved, and at times that's true. The seller might be willing to sell the house for less if they do not have to pay Realtor fees, or they may choose to maximize their own profits. Every transaction is different.

How to Find a Great Agent

Exclusive Buyer Agents can be hard to find. If you can't find one in your area, you may be forced to work with a traditional agent that represents both buyers and sellers, or who is a self-proclaimed buyer agent. My company has agents in Dallas, Austin, and Houston, but I'd be happy to help you find a buyer friendly agent in your area. Send your request to Alysse@HelpUBuyAmerica.com.

If you're forced to hire a regular buyer agent, don't share too much information with them! You never know when they are going to switch to the other side.

If they have a listing in your price range, they are almost certainly going to show it to you, since this will allow them to earn both sides of the commission. The buyer's negotiating position is highly compromised in this type of office, and a truly level playing field only exists when the buyer works with a single agent. Share what you must but keep some things to yourself, like how much home you can afford, how much cash you have in the bank, and how desperate you are to move out of your apartment.

Treat the Realtor as a friendly adversary, not as someone you can trust with your money!

Interviewing Agents

Always meet a prospective agent before you decide to work with them; a phone interview is not enough. The agent/buyer relationship can be a long one, and the two personalities need to "click" to a certain degree. Imagine spending weeks looking at homes with someone you don't like (or who doesn't like you). Here are some questions you need to ask prospective agents:

How long have you been in business?

Because the buyer assumes the risk in a real estate transaction, you need an agent with at least 3-5 years' experience, or a new agent that works very closely with their broker. The broker and the agent should work as a team.

Whom do you represent?

Most agents will say that they represent both buyers and sellers. Some will say that even though they work in a traditional real estate office, *they* only work with buyers, or that *they* are their office's buyer specialist.

> *The truth is that it doesn't matter what they say; if they are not an EBA, they represent both sides. It is imperative that I make this point clear.*

Texas Realtors are required by law to give you a document called "Information about Brokerage Services" at your first substantive meeting. This form is a disclosure that discusses the various types of agency (buyer, seller, dual/intermediary). This is your opportunity to discuss this important issue in greater detail.

How do you handle competing buyers?

What happens if the agent has a buyer who is looking for the same type of house as one of their other buyers? Who gets the first look at the property, and what happens if both buyers want to make an offer? My personal policy is that I don't take on two clients looking for exactly the same property. Be clear on your agent's policy.

How do you handle in-house listings?

There are incentives for Re/Max agents, for example, to show Re/Max listed homes. How do they handle representing both the buyer and seller in the same transaction? Are you going to be turned over to another agent to handle your negotiations? It's imperative that you know and understand their procedures, and don't let them convince you that it's not a big deal. It is.

How will you notify me of new listings?

Most offices have some kind of auto-search capability, which automatically sends new listings to their clients the moment they are entered in the

MLS. Buyers can go online and look at pictures, take virtual tours, and make notes about homes they like. It helps all parties to communicate about specific homes and to stay organized.

How much notice do you need for appointments?

A successful career agent isn't going to be available at the drop of a hat to show you a home. I schedule my weekend showings five or six days in advance, but am often more flexible during the week. I also have an assistant who can show a home for me in case of emergency. Find out how your prospective agent works.

How do you get paid?

Commissions are negotiable, but many residential buyer agents work for 3% of the sales price, and the fee is deducted from the seller's proceeds at closing. Some Realtors charge buyers an upfront retainer, which is fully refundable at closing. Realtors often use retainers to eliminate buyers who are time wasters. I often collect a small deposit ($100), but there are many agents who will be inexperienced or desperate enough to drive you around and show you houses for free. Others want their gas money upfront.

Can I review copies of your paperwork?

Don't feel pressured into signing a buyer's representation agreement on the spot. Take it home, review it, and negotiate the terms with which you don't agree. These agreements are discussed further later in this chapter.

What happens to bonuses that are offered to the selling agent?

If the sellers are offering to pay a $5,000 bonus to the agent who brings them a buyer, what happens to this money? Some agents will state that they can keep the bonus as long as it is disclosed to all parties. *Don't hire this agent! You must be able to trust that the advice they give you is independent of any additional financial incentive.* Our policy is to rebate all bonuses and money in excess of the negotiated commission back to the buyer. That should be your policy too.

What happens if the seller only offers two percent to the buyer's agent, but yours works for three percent?

This happens sometimes with bank-owned properties or sellers who have little equity in their home. Are you willing to pay your agent the extra one percent by rolling it into the price of the home? Will you pay the agent in cash? If not, do you want your agent to even show you homes that offer less than a three percent commission? This is an important issue and you would do well to make your wishes known.

Meaningless Questions

You can ask the following questions, if you like, but don't put too much stock in their answers.

Do you have references?

All agents have references, but it doesn't necessarily mean those references are meaningful or even real. Even the reviews you read online aren't necessarily accurate. Visit the Texas Real Estate Commission's (TREC) website (http://www.trec.state.tx.us/) to see if they have been disciplined for any reason. Get a referral from a friend if you can, but always have an exit strategy or a plan to end the relationship if it is not working out.

Can you give me a list of buyer clients with their addresses and how much they saved?

An agent who would give you this information is not very smart. I would never compromise my client's safety and privacy in order to get a new client. New homeowners become the target of many, many scams, and I'm not going to inadvertently become part of a transaction that harms my clients. Find an agent who has integrity and concern for things other than their own pock-etbook.

How much of a discount can you usually get off the price of a home?

There are far too many variables for anyone to be able to answer this question accurately, and any answer you receive would be a complete guess or a complete lie. Price is only one of many possible seller concessions. And, if five buyers are competing for the same house, you want the agent that is going to be able to convince the seller's side to sell the house to you, not one of the other four buyers. You need an agent who can present your offer in a way that wins you the house, and often it has nothing to do with money.

Buyer Representation Agreements

A buyer's representation agreement is an employment contract that spells out the duties and responsibilities of the Realtor to the buyer, and vice versa. Most Realtors will want you to sign one. In fact, some won't show you a home until they have you under contract. Realtors want to ensure they will be paid for the work that they do, and it is unfair for a buyer to use their services to tour houses only to switch Realtors or buy the home through a discounter at the last minute.

Pictured below is the six-page Buyer's Representation Agreement used by most Texas Realtors. When a Realtor tells you they are a buyer's agent even though they work for a company that takes listings, this is the document that they use (or one very similar).

RESIDENTIAL BUYER/TENANT REPRESENTATION AGREEMENT
Austin Board of REALTORS®

THIS FORM IS FURNISHED BY THE AUSTIN BOARD OF REALTORS® FOR USE BY ITS PARTICIPANTS.
USE OF THIS FORM BY PERSONS WHO ARE NOT PARTICIPANTS OF THE
AUSTIN BOARD OF REALTORS® IS NOT AUTHORIZED.

1. **PARTIES:** The parties to this Buyer/Tenant Representation Agreement are:

    Buyer/Client: <u>**Mr. Buyer**</u>
    <u>**Mrs. Buyer**</u>
    Address: _____
    City, State, Zip: _____
    Phone: <u>**(555) 123-4567**</u> Cell: _____ Fax: _____
    E-Mail: <u>**mrbuyer@me.com**</u>

    Broker: _____
    Broker's Address: _____
    Broker's Associate: _____
    City, State, Zip: _____
    Phone: _____ Cell: _____ Fax: _____
    E-Mail: _____

2. **APPOINTMENT:** Buyer grants to Broker the <u>**sole and exclusive right**</u> to act as Client's real estate agent for the purpose of acquiring property in the market area. All notices shall be in writing and effective when hand-delivered, mailed or sent by facsimile or electronic transmission to the above.

3. **DEFINITIONS:**

    A. *"Acquire"* means to purchase or lease.

    B. *"Closing"* in a sale transaction means the date legal title to a property is conveyed to a purchaser of property under a contract to buy. *"Closing"* in a lease transaction means the date a landlord and tenant enter into a binding lease of a property.

    C. *"Market area"* means that area in the State of Texas within the perimeter boundaries of the following areas:
    _____
    _____

4. **TERM:** This Agreement commences on _____ and ends at 11:59 P.M.
    on _____ .

5. **BROKER'S OBLIGATIONS:**

    A. Broker will use Broker's best efforts to assist Client in acquiring property in the market area;

    B. Broker will assist Client in negotiating the acquisition of property in the market area; and

    C. Broker will comply with other provisions of this agreement.

6. **CLIENT'S OBLIGATIONS:**

    A. Client will work exclusively through Broker in acquiring property in the market area and negotiate the acquisition of property in the market area only through Broker;

    B. Client will inform other Brokers, salespersons, sellers, and landlords with whom Client may have contact that Broker exclusively represents Client for the purpose of acquiring property in the market area and refer all such persons to Broker; and

    C. Client will comply with other provisions of this Agreement.

Initialed for Identification by Broker/Associate _____ and Buyer _____ , _____   Page 1 of 6

© 2006 Austin Board of REALTORS®
HelpUBuy America, 106 N. Denton Tap Road Coppell, TX 75019
Phone: 214.734.3863   Fax: 866-593-9533   Alysse Musgrave   Book
Produced with ZipForm® by zipLogix 18070 Fifteen Mile Road, Fraser, Michigan 48026 www.zipLogix.com

The "market area" is often defined by contiguous counties. The "term" is generally for a period of six months.

Buyer/Tenant Representation Agreement between _____

and _____

7. REPRESENTATIONS:

A. Each person signing this Agreement represents that the person has the legal capacity and authority to bind the respective party to this Agreement.

B. Client represents that Client is not now a party to another buyer or tenant representation agreement with another broker for the acquisition of property in the market area.

C. Client represents that all information relating to Client's ability to acquire property in the market area Client gives to Broker is true and correct.

D. Name any employer, relocation company, or other entity that will provide benefits to Client when acquiring property in the market area: _____

8. INTERMEDIARY: *(Check A or B only.)*

Notice: **If Broker acts as an Intermediary under Paragraph 8.A., Broker and Broker's Associates:**

- **May not disclose to Client that the Seller or Landlord will accept a price less than the asking price unless otherwise instructed in a separate writing by the Seller or Landlord;**
- **May not disclose to the Seller or Landlord that Client will pay a price greater than the price submitted in a written offer to the Seller or Landlord unless otherwise instructed in a separate writing by Client;**
- **May not disclose any confidential information or any information a Seller or Landlord or Client specifically instructs Broker in writing not to disclose unless otherwise instructed in a separate writing by the respective party or required to disclose the information by the Real Estate License Act or a court order or if the information materially relates to the condition of the property.**
- **Shall treat all parties to the transaction honestly; and**
- **Shall comply with the Real Estate License Act.**

☐ A. <u>Intermediary Status:</u> Client desires to see Broker's listings. If Client wishes to acquire one of Broker's listings, Client authorizes Broker to act as an Intermediary and Broker will notify Client that Broker will service the parties in accordance with one of the following alternatives:

(1) If the Owner of the property is serviced by an Associate other than the Associate servicing Client under this Agreement, Broker may notify Client that Broker will:

(a) Appoint the Associate then servicing the Owner to communicate with, carry out instructions of, and provide opinions and advice during negotiations to the Owner; and

(b) Appoint the Associate then servicing the Client to the Client for the same purpose.

(2) If the Owner of the property is serviced by the same Associate who is servicing Client, Broker may notify Client that Broker will:

(a) Appoint another Associate to communicate with, carry out instructions of, and provide opinions and advice during negotiations to Client; and

(b) Appoint the Associate servicing the Owner under the listing to the Owner for the same purpose.

(3) Broker may notify Client that Broker will make no appointments as described under this Paragraph 8A and, in such event, the Associate servicing the parties will act solely as Broker's Intermediary Representative, who may facilitate the transaction **but will not render opinions or advice during negotiations to either party**.

☐ B. <u>No Intermediary Status:</u> Client does not wish to be shown or acquire any of Broker's listings.

Initialed for Identification by Broker/Associate _____ and Buyer _____ , _____   Page 2 of 6

© 2006 Austin Board of REALTORS®

Book

Produced with ZipForm® by zipLogix 18070 Fifteen Mile Road, Fraser, Michigan 48026 www.zipLogix.com

This section introduces intermediary status. If you happen to fall in love with one of the Broker's in-house listings, you forfeit your right to buyer representation. The Broker will no longer give you their opinion or advice during negotiations. If this makes you uncomfortable (and it should), you can choose not to view or purchase any of the Broker's listings, leaving you with a more limited amount of inventory from which to choose a home.

Buyer/Tenant Representation Agreement between _____

and _____

9.   COMPETING CLIENTS: Client acknowledges that Broker may represent other prospective buyers or tenants who may seek to acquire properties that may be of interest to Client. Client agrees that Broker may, during the term of this Agreement and after it ends, represent such other prospects, show the other prospects the same properties that Broker shows to Client, and act as a real estate broker for such other prospects in negotiating the acquisition of properties that Client may seek to acquire. Broker will not disclose the price offered or financial details of Client's offer to other potential buyers nor will Broker disclose to Client the details of any other offer presented by another buyer represented by Broker.

10.   CONFIDENTIAL INFORMATION:

   A.   During the term of this Agreement or after its termination, Broker may not knowingly disclose information obtained in confidence from Client except as authorized by Client or required by law. Broker may not disclose to Client any information obtained in confidence regarding any other person Broker represents or may have represented except as required by law.

   B.   Client hereby acknowledges that sellers or sellers' representatives may not treat the existence, terms, or conditions of offers as confidential unless confidentiality is required by law, regulation, or by any confidentiality agreement between the parties.

11.   BROKER'S FEES:

   A.   Professional Fees:

   (1)   Commission: The parties agree that Broker will receive a commission calculated as follows:

   (a)   _____ % of the gross sales price if Client agrees to purchase property in the market area; and

   (b)   if Client agrees to lease property in the market area a fee equal to (check only one box):

   ☐   _____ % of one month's rent or

   ☐   _____ % of all rents to be paid over the term of the lease.

   (2)   Retainer: Upon execution of this Agreement, Client will pay Broker a retainer of $ _____ .
   The Retainer is earned at the time it is paid.

   (3)   Hourly Fees: Client will pay Broker fees at the rate of $ _____ per hour. Broker's hourly fees are earned when Broker's services are rendered and are payable when billed.

   (4)   Other: _____
   _____

   B.   Source of Commission Payment: Broker will seek to obtain payment of the commission specified in Paragraph 11A(1) first from the Seller, Landlord, or their agents. If such persons refuse or fail to pay Broker the amount specifed, Client will pay Broker the amount specified less any amounts Broker receives from such persons.

The page above gives the broker permission to work with other buyers who are looking for the same kind of property as you. They can act in your best interest to help *you* make an offer on the home of your choice and later help their *other* client negotiate against you.

Section 10 states that the Broker may not *knowingly* disclose information obtained in confidence, but disclosing information *accidentally on purpose* is okay. Section 11 stipulates that if the seller doesn't agree to pay the broker's commission, the buyer must pay the fee.

Buyer/Tenant Representation Agreement between _____

and _____

C. **Earned and Payable:** A person is not obligated to pay Broker a commission until such time as Broker's commission is *earned and payable.* Broker's commission is earned when:

(1) Client enters into a contract to buy or lease property in the market area; or

(2) Client breaches this Agreement.

Broker's commission is *payable,* either during the term of this Agreement or after it ends, upon the earlier of:

(1) the closing of the transaction to acquire the property;

(2) Client's breach of a contract to buy or lease a property in the market area; or

(3) Client's breach of this Agreement.

If Client acquires more than one property under this agreement, Broker's commissions for each property acquired are earned as each property is acquired and are payable at the closing of each acquisition.

D. **Additional Compensation:** If a Seller, Landlord, or their agents offer compensation in excess of the amount stated in Paragraph 11.A.(1) (including but not limited to marketing incentives or bonuses to cooperating brokers) Broker may retain the additional compensation in addition to the specified commission. **Broker shall disclose the source and amount of any additional compensation to client when known.** Client is not obligated to pay any such additional compensation to Broker.

E. **Acquisition of Broker's Listing:** Notwithstanding any provision to the contrary, if Client acquires a property listed by Broker, Broker will be paid in accordance with the terms of Broker's Listing Agreement with the Owner and Client will have no obligation to pay Broker.

F. In addition to the commission specified under Paragraph 11.A.(1), Broker is entitled to the following fees:

(1) **Custom Construction:** If Client uses Broker's services for new construction on property owned by Client, Client will a) pay the fee listed below or b) direct the contractor providing construction services to pay the fee listed below to Broker when construction on property owned by Client is substantially complete.

_____

(2) **Service Providers:** If Broker refers Client or any party to a transaction contemplated by this Agreement to a service provider (i.e., mover, cable company, telecommunications provider, utility, or contractor) Broker may receive a fee from the service provider for the referral.

(3) **Other:** _____

G. **Protection Period:** *Protection period* means that time starting the day after this Agreement ends and continuing for _____ days. Not later than 10 days after this Agreement ends, Broker may send Client written notice identifying the properties called to Client's attention during this agreement. If Client or a relative of Client agrees to acquire a property identified in the notice during the protection period, Client will pay Broker, upon closing, the amount Broker would have been entitled to receive if this Agreement were still in effect. This Paragraph 11.G. survives termination of this Agreement. This Paragraph 11.G. will not apply if Client is, during the protection period, bound under a representation agreement with another broker who is a member of the Austin Board of REALTORS® at the time the acquisition is negotiated and the other broker is paid a fee for negotiating the transaction.

H. **Escrow Authorization:** Client authorizes, and Broker may so instruct, any escrow or closing agent authorized to close a transaction for the acquisition of property contemplated by this Agreement to collect and disburse to Broker all amounts payable to Broker.

I. **County:** Amounts payable to Broker are to be paid in cash in _____ County, Texas.

Initialed for Identification by Broker/Associate _____ and Buyer _____ , _____   Page 4 of 6

© 2006 Austin Board of REALTORS®

Produced with ZipForm® by zipLogix 18070 Fifteen Mile Road, Fraser, Michigan 48026 www.zipLogix.com

Book

Earned & payable means the broker gets paid even if you buy a house that they didn't show you, or if they do lousy job. Seem fair? The additional compensation section stipulates that the Broker can keep any sales incentives or bonuses offered by the seller of a property, as long as they make the proper disclosure. Section F2 states that the Broker is allowed to receive kickbacks from the cable company, warranty providers, movers, etc.

Buyer/Tenant Representation Agreement between _____

and _____

12. **MEDIATION:** The parties agree to negotiate in good faith in an effort to resolve any dispute that may arise related to this Agreement or any transaction related to or contemplated by this Agreement. If the dispute cannot be resolved by negotiation, the parties will submit the dispute to mediation before resorting to arbitration or litigation and will equally share the costs of a mutually acceptable mediator.

13. **TERMINATION:** The parties' agency relationship can be terminated at any time; however, the contractual provisions and obligations will survive and can only be modified or terminated by the mutual consent of both parties.

14. **DEFAULT:** If either party fails to comply with this Agreement or makes a false representation in this Agreement, the non-complying party is in default. If Client is in default, Client will be liable for the amount of compensation that Broker would have received under this Agreement if Client was not in default. If Broker is in default, Client may exercise any remedy at law.

15. **ATTORNEY'S FEES:** If Client or Broker is a prevailing party in any legal proceeding brought as a result of a dispute under this Agreement or any transaction related to this Agreement, such party shall recover from the non-prevailing party all costs of such proceeding and reasonable attorney's fees.

16. **LIMITATION OF LIABILITY:** Neither Broker nor any other broker, or their associates, is responsible or liable for Client's personal injuries or for any loss or damage to Client's property that is not caused by Broker. Client will hold broker, any other broker, and their associates, harmless from any such injuries or losses. Client will indemnify Broker against any claims for injury or damage that Client may cause to others or their property.

17. **ADDENDA:** The Information About Brokerage Services (TREC Form OP-K) is attached and incorporated into this Agreement by reference. Addenda and other related documents which are part of this Agreement are:
    - ☐ Protect Your Family from Lead in Your Home (TAR 2511)
    - ☐ Protecting Your Home from Mold (TAR 2507)
    - ☐ Information about Special Flood Hazard Areas (TAR 1414)
    - ☐ Information About Property Insurance (TAR 2508)
    - ☐ For Your Protection: Get a Home Inspection (TAR 1928) - FOR FHA TRANSACTIONS ONLY
    - ☐ General Information and Notice to a Buyer (TAR 1506)
    - ☐ Other: _____

18. **SPECIAL PROVISIONS:**

19. **ADDITIONAL NOTICES:**

    A. Broker's fees or the sharing of fees between Brokers are not fixed, controlled, recommended, suggested, or maintained by the Austin Board of REALTORS®, the Texas Association of REALTORS®, MLS, or any listing service.

    B. Broker's services are provided without regard to race, color, religion, national origin, sex, disability, or familial status. Local ordinances may provide for additional protected classes, i.e., creed, status as a student, marital status, sexual orientation, or age.

    When involved in the sale or lease of a residence, REALTORS® shall not volunteer information regarding the racial, religious or ethnic composition of any neighborhood nor shall they engage in any activity which may result in panic selling, however, REALTORS® may provide other demographic information.

Initialed for Identification by Broker/Associate _____ and Buyer _____ , _____   Page 5 of 6

Book

The termination clause states that the contract can be terminated at any time, but all the terms remain in effect unless both parties agree to terminate the terms.

Buyer/Tenant Representation Agreement between _____
and _____

    C. Broker is not a property inspector, surveyor, engineer, environmental assessor, or compliance inspector. Client should seek experts to render such services in any acquisition.

    D. If Client purchases property, Client should have an abstract covering the property examined by an attorney of Client's selection, or Client should be furnished with or obtain a title policy.

    E. Buyer may purchase a Residential Service Contract. Buyer should review such service contract for the scope of coverage, exclusions, and limitations. The purchase of a Residential Service Contract is optional. There are several residential service companies operating in Texas.

    F. In response to inquiries from Buyers or cooperating Brokers, REALTORS® shall, with sellers' approval, disclose the existence of offers on the property. Where disclosure is authorized, REALTORS® shall also disclose whether offers were obtained by the listing licensee, another licensee in the listing firm, or by a cooperating broker.

    G. Broker cannot give legal advice. This is a legally binding Agreement. READ IT CAREFULLY. If you do not understand the effect of this Agreement, consult your attorney, BEFORE signing.

The remaining clauses hold the broker harmless from liability for injuries and damages incurred on or to the property, and recommends that the buyer hire proper inspectors to evaluate the condition of the property before finalizing the purchase.

As you can see, this agreement provides far more protection for the broker than for the buyer. There is nothing that guarantees client satisfaction or that protects you from an unskilled or unethical agent. It doesn't list their duties or discuss their responsibilities toward you.

Don't be afraid to dictate the terms of this agreement. Here are some ways you can tweak your contract with your agent:

- Instead of committing to a six-month agreement, adopt a one-month agreement with an option to renew at a later time. This will give you some time to get to know your agent before making a long-term commitment to them.
- Have the commitment apply only to the houses that they show you, and omit any mention of a time period.
- Designate a trial period, after which the full agreement goes into effect unless either party terminates the agreement.
- Most importantly, always insist on an "out" clause so that you can be released at any time. The agent will only be paid on homes that they have shown you, should you choose to buy one of those homes. A good agent is going to have some sort of customer satisfaction guarantee. If they don't, find someone else.

I personally don't use this type of buyer's representation agreement. In fact, I don't even ask a buyer to sign one. I'm confident in my skills. If a buyer/client doesn't want to work with me, they are free to go at any time with no strings attached. Working with me should be the least stressful part of the homebuying process. It's not unreasonable for you to expect the same from the agent you hire.

If It's Not Working Out

If you begin to work with an agent and find that it's not a good fit, you're not stuck. Don't be intimidated by a scary buyer's representation agreement. Before you fire them, however, first make sure your expectations are reasonable.

Your agent isn't your companion or tour guide; their job is to help you buy a house, not to take you to lunch. Don't expect them to drop everything and show you a house at the last minute. Show up on time for all your appointments since tours have to be scheduled with the seller, and don't expect calls to be returned at all hours of the night. This isn't a volunteer job for agents; it's how we support our families and put our kids through college. A new agent anxious to build their career might put up with this kind of thing for a while, but an experienced agent will drop you like a bad habit.

If your agent hasn't shown you houses in a couple of weeks, ask why. It is possible that your search criterion is too narrow and that there is nothing to show. Agents deserve the opportunity to explain themselves, and it is easier to give them a chance than it is to start over with a new agent. If you have expressed your concerns to the agent and you are still unhappy, it's time to fire them.

How to Fire Your Agent

If your agent has shown you a home that you wish to buy, but you have some concerns about their skills or level of knowledge, contact their broker (boss) and ask to have another agent assigned to you. The released agent will be fairly compensated for their time when the transaction closes.

If you haven't found a house through this agent, review the agreement you signed and determine the terms of the "out" clause. You must send written notification that terminates the relationship. Send the letter to both the agent and the broker and see what happens. There's no reason to be insulting or antagonistic. Simply state that your plans have changed and that you wish to terminate the agreement. They can't force you to make an offer or buy a house through them. In fact, a Realtor is not even entitled to receive a commission on a transaction unless they are the "procuring cause" (instigated the transaction) of the sale, regardless of what the agreement says. Most brokers won't sue a buyer for terminating the buyer's representation agreement. But if you have a Realtor show you homes all over town, let them research and negotiate the purchase of particular home, and later buy the home on your own or with another agent, you can be sued and *you will lose*! Beware bad real estate karma. You have been warned.

{ 2 }

Getting Started

Buying a home is both a business decision and an emotional one, or it should be. It's a lot of fun to go online and take virtual tours and visit open houses, but when you're ready to make a move, it's time for a more methodical approach.

Pre-Qualifying vs. Pre-Approval

Getting pre-qualified is the very first step in the homebuying process and is more than likely the first requirement of any Realtor you hire. A quick call to a lender will determine your buying power, your cash on hand requirements, and will identify suitable loan programs. Many buyers mistakenly believe that if they have been pre-qualified for a loan, they are pre-approved. This isn't true. There is a big difference between the two, as discussed below.

Pre-Qualifying

Pre-qualifying for a loan is simple and straightforward. You supply a lender with your overall financial picture, including your credit score, debt, income, and assets. After evaluating this information, a lender will give you an idea of the mortgage amount for which you qualify. Pre-qualification can be done over the phone or on the Internet and there is usually no cost involved.

At this point, a lender can only explain your options and make recommendations. Because it is based only on the information *you* provide to the lender and because this information isn't verified, your loan approval is not guaranteed; it's just the amount for which you might expect to be approved and an estimate of your projected monthly payment. Being pre-qualified doesn't carry the same weight as being pre-approved, which is discussed next.

Pre-Approval

Getting pre-approved tends to be much more involved than getting pre-qualified. You'll complete an official mortgage application and send the lender the necessary documentation to verify your qualifications. Your credit will be checked, and the loan officer may make recommendations on ways to improve your credit score so that you can qualify for a lower interest rate. At this point, you might not have found a house yet, so any reference to a specific property on the application will be left blank. The lender can tell you with certainty the specific mortgage amount for which you are approved, and you'll have a better idea of the interest rate you will be charged. You'll receive a written, conditional commitment, which is what you need before you put an offer on a house. Once you have this letter in hand, you're ready to start shopping for a home.

Wants Versus Needs

There is a lot to consider when shopping for a home, including location, budget, property condition, schools, resale, floor plan, potential appreciation vs. depreciation, and much more. It's best to start by making a list of items that are appealing to you and then ranking them in order of importance. Do this before you start to look at homes so that unimportant things, like décor, do not distract you. The following are some things to consider before you start to look at homes.

Bedrooms and Bathrooms

The safest size single-family home is a four-bedroom. For resale purposes, anyone who can fit into a three-bedroom home would fit into a four-bedroom home. The opposite is not true. A family who needs a four-bedroom home would never consider a three-bedroom home. If a four-bedroom home is not in your budget, three bedrooms are perfectly fine. Be mindful of the size and functionality of the shared living space and be sure there is a space for a home office, since this is a "must have" for many homebuyers these days.

One- or Two-Story Home

There are both advantages and disadvantages to either a one-story or a two-story home. In a one-story home, the ceilings can be higher and there is no noise from people walking overhead. It is easier and safer for small children and the elderly or disabled to live on one floor, and you don't have wasted space where the stairs would go. On the down side, the yard is usually smaller due to the larger footprint of the house. There is typically less privacy and the bedrooms are often smaller.

Living in a two-story home usually means nice views from the second floor and more separation between living spaces and bedrooms. It's safe to leave windows open on the second floor, the yard is sometimes larger, and if all the bedrooms are upstairs, you don't have to heat or cool the first floor while you are sleeping. The negatives are the noise level when people are walking on the second floor and the stairs, which can be inconvenient or pro-hibitive if a family member becomes injured or sick

Number of living areas

Most of my clients are very happy not to have a formal living area, opting instead for a home office. The family room is typically where everyone gath-ers, so make sure this space is on the larger side, and be mindful of traffic patterns once all the furniture is in place. You typically need a 3' wide walkway to move from space to space. If you have children and want them to have a separate space for their toys and friends, be sure to find a home with at least two living areas. Many people like to have a separate game room just for the kids and their mess.

Number of dining areas

Although people don't use their formal living space anymore, there is still a strong demand for a formal dining room; it is preferable to have a mini-mum of two eating areas. Most meals will be in the breakfast room, so it is important that this space is large enough to accommodate a table and at least four chairs comfortably. If the door to the back yard is in the breakfast room, be sure that there will be room to open the door once the dinette is in place. The dining room should accommodate a minimum of six people. The only exception to this rule applies to townhomes, where a single dining room is somewhat common.

Garage spaces

In many parts of the country, single-family homes come with a two-car garage. You may encounter homes where the homeowners have converted the garage into living space. Be sure that the space can be converted back to a garage easily, since homes without garages are harder to sell. If you are purchasing a home in a neighborhood where most of the homes have a three-car garage, do not buy a home with a two-car garage.

You want your house to blend with the other homes in the neigh-borhood.

Square Feet

It's smart to have a general idea of what 3000 square feet looks and feels like, but don't get too concerned about numbers. The floor plan matters more than the square footage of a house. A good floor plan can make a 2500 square foot home feel like a palace. Conversely, a 4000 square foot home can feel small if there is not enough usable space or if the design is poor. If you think you want a 3000 square foot home, let your Realtor show you homes in the 2700-3300 square foot range. You never know when a house you tour will be *the* house, even though it wasn't perfect on paper.

Age of home

If you are concerned about energy conservation and your utility bills, newer is better - by far. The cost to cool a home built in the 1980s can be triple the cost to cool the same size home built in the year 2000 or later. Improvements in the quality of insulation, windows, roof decking/radiant barriers, energy star appliances, and air conditioners have substantially reduced the cost to heat and cool a home. Sacrifices are to be made, however. Older homes were typically built on bigger, and sometimes more beautiful lots, and they have a much different look and feel than new homes (for better or for worse). If you are not sure of your preference, I suggest that you have your agent show you a few older homes. You will know right away if older homes are something you wish to consider.

Area

Decide where you want to live before you hire an agent, but be open to any suggestions that they may have. How far are you willing to drive to get to work? Do you want to be close to downtown, or are you happy in the suburbs? Schools are always an important consideration, and you should buy a home in a decent school district, even if you don't have children. Find out where the good schools are and then take a ride to that area. Or go online, find some homes in your price range, and drive around those neighborhoods to see how you like them.

An afternoon in the car can answer a lot of questions for you.

Yard Size

A large yard generally means more maintenance. If you are not willing to do the work yourself, make sure you have the money to hire someone to take care of it for you. Generally speaking, people like a larger yard. Unless you are buying a townhouse, don't buy a house with the smallest yard in the neighborhood; you may have a hard time selling the property. Play the averages and find a home that has an average size lot or bigger.

Price range

There is a big difference between how much money the bank will lend you, how much you can truly afford, and how much you should be willing to spend. Just because the bank will lend you $400,000, doesn't mean you should borrow that much. Consider the monthly cost of utilities, repairs, cleaning, maintenance, and furniture. Bankrate.com has some great mortgage calculators to help you decide how much home you can comfortably afford.

Aim to buy everything you need, but just some of the things you want. There is a difference.

Property Condition

How much work are you willing to do? You might be open to making cosmetic changes like paint, carpet, etc., but it is important to know your limits. If you are going to make changes to the property before you move in, be sure that you have the money for both labor and materials, even if you plan to do the work yourself. And it's really important to have some "oops" money set aside, just in case.

Pool

People don't always realize the work and money involved with maintaining a pool. The costs include heating, cleaning, chemicals, insurance, and there is the constant concern about the safety of your children, pets, and even the neighborhood children. If you are not 100 percent certain that you want a pool, my advice is to not get one. However, if you know for certain that you want one, it is much smarter to buy a home with a pool already installed. If you add a pool later, it is likely you will only recuperate about 50 percent of your original cost, at best, when you decide to sell the home.

Working With Your Agent

Sharing your wants and needs with your Realtor will expedite the process and save you from looking at a lot of homes that won't work for you. Your agent can then send you a list of homes that suit your needs and you can make arrangements to visit the ones that are most appealing. If your list seems very brief, your requirements may not be reasonable. But don't automatically assume that you need to increase the price. Tweak some of the other criteria first, like square feet, and see what compromises may need to be made.

I like to have my buyer/clients choose the homes that interest them, at least initially. It helps me learn their likes and dislikes, and allows me the opportunity to learn what appeals to them. I am always looking at For Sale By Owner (FSBO) homes and new construction, and I need to be able to recognize my buyer's dream home when I see it. I've heard buyers complain that their Realtors were not working for them when they send them lists of homes to review. This is nonsense!

You and your Realtor have the same goal: To help you find your dream home. They can't find you what you want if they don't know what that is. Communicate with your Realtor and don't judge his or her ability based on this part of the process.

> *Anyone can open a door and schedule a showing. It is that which comes after the house is found that makes a good Realtor invaluable.*

MLS Listed Homes

More than likely you will receive MLS listings via email, and there will be links to view photos and to take virtual tours. Lots of agents use services that will send you new listings automatically so you will know what's new on the market in real time. Mine is an online gateway that buyers can use to sort through the listings and communicate with me about the homes that appeal to them. I strongly suggest that you hire an agent who takes advantage of all the available technology. It makes the process easier, more efficient, and a lot more fun.

For Sale by Owners (FSBOs)

FSBOs are homes being marketed without the help of an agent; they are not always listed on the MLS, but your agent can still help you purchase a home that is for sale by owner. A home is for sale by owner for one of these reasons:

- The homeowner hates Realtors.
- They think they can do a lot of what a seller's agent does on their own, without paying a six percent commission.
- The homeowners do not have enough equity in the home to pay Realtor fees, so they have no choice but to sell it themselves.

FSBOs have more options than ever when it comes to selling their homes. In the past, in order to get their home listed on the MLS, homeowners had no choice but to hire a Realtor to represent them and pay a five or six percent commission. These days, they can pay $100- $500 and have their home listed on the MLS. Once listed, every Realtor in that area can view the listing and show the home to prospective buyers. The seller offers a commission to the Realtor that brings the buyer, and the seller pays about half of what they normally would in commissions. This is a very smart way to sell a home, in some cases, as long as they make it easy for Realtors to show the house.

Secret: Realtors hate working with FSBOs

Why? Homeowners typically don't know how to value their property and the home is often priced incorrectly. I *love* finding a great house for sale by owner that is priced far too low, and it thrills me when my clients get a great deal. But, more often than not, the house is overpriced and working with the seller is difficult at best. I work with FSBOs all the time, but I hate it. Most will not use a lockbox, making it necessary for the seller to provide access to the property. That means I have to make an appointment with the seller directly, versus one call to a service that makes all my appointments for me, and then coordinate that time with the buyer. When I call the owner to schedule an appointment, they are always suspicious of me and generally grumpy because so many listing agents have contacted them trying to list their home. The seller insists on showing us around the house and it's awkward, since most buyers don't feel comfortable opening doors and looking in closets when the seller is present. The showing takes three times longer than usual because the seller wants to make small talk and woo the buyers. In addition, the homes are seldom worth considering because they did not have a Realtor advising them on the best way to present their home to buyers. Yes, I *hate* working with FSBOs.

Still, I always look for FSBOs for my clients, but not right away. Once I have a really good idea of what my buyers are looking for and where, I preview by owner homes and only take my clients to see the strong possibilities. I also do a quick Comparative Market Analysis (CMA) to see how the home is priced, and I try to get as much information about the seller and the house as possible, in case my client decides to make an offer. The seller needs to have an idea of how real estate is sold in my state because I'm not their agent, and it is not my job to help them sell their house.

> *I will not let my buyers spend a dime until I am convinced that the seller will actually close the deal.*

After all, the seller has nothing to lose. My buyer pays for inspections and appraisals, and they will lose hundreds of dollars if the seller doesn't close. It is my job to ensure that doesn't happen. So if your Realtor is not showing you FSBOs, do not assume it's because they are lazy or that they are trying to hide something from you. Sometimes they are protecting you from a seller who has no idea what they are doing.

New Construction

There are some advantages to buying a brand new home. First, there is the "new house smell" and the fact that no one else's feet have ever been on your carpet. More importantly, new homes offer energy saving features unmatched by homes even a few years old. A new home generally has a ten-year transferrable structural warranty, which includes foundation and load bearing items, a two-year systems warranty including electrical, plumbing, and air conditioning, and a one-year floor to ceiling warranty. However, for every positive there is a negative, and the negatives range from superficial to deal killer.

You generally pay a premium for new construction, and it can take about five years before you really start to build any equity in your home. Builders start new communities where there is open land, and that generally means that your commute is going to be longer and that you will be farther away from the center of the city. When the neighborhood is new, you really won't know what type of neighbors you will have until after you move in. The biggest risk, however, involves the condition of the house. It may take a year or more before you notice defects in the property. In my area, the risk is caused by our clay-based soil, which leads to a large number of foundation problems. In your area, it may be something different, but the assumption that homes are free of problems simply because they are new is wrong, wrong, wrong.

Types of New Homes

There are three different types of new construction homes: custom homes, spec homes, and tract homes, discussed below.

Custom Homes

When building a custom home, you make all the choices. You pick the lot, the builder, the architect, faucets, roof, air conditioning, and everything in between.

On the plus side, you get *almost* exactly what you want, and you have some control of the price, at least in theory. You move into a home that does not look like every home on the block, and you can take pride in the fact that you conceptualized your vision and saw it through to fruition.

Now - the down side. The first obstacle is finding a builder that can deliver everything they promise. You have to worry about the builder going over budget, running off with your money, going bankrupt, whether or not they can find quality labor to construct your home, and whether or not your marriage will survive the process. Chances are they will not finish on time, and in the end you will probably only get 95 percent of what you wanted.

Theoretically, you could use a Realtor as a second set of eyes and ears, but you probably will not find one dumb enough to get involved.

Tract Homes

Developers who buy a large piece of land and divide it up into much smaller lots build what are known as "tract" homes and create subdivisions. When you think tract home, you might think David Weekley, Meritage Homes, Ryland Homes, First Texas, and others. Generally, the builder has 15-20 floor plans that they build in a subdivision, and they are all similar, but not identical. You pick one of the floor plans, choose your cosmetic items, customize the floor plan (depending on the builder), and six months later you have a house. Because of the volume of homes being built and the lower costs of materials and labor, tract homes are generally far less expensive than custom homes. The price and availability are the most appealing things about tract homes. However, you should know that the quality varies not only by builder, but also by area. Do not assume that Bob's Fancy Homes, for example, builds the same quality product in all parts of town. The price point and their desired profit margin dictate the quality of the materials that they use, and in some areas the quality is *horrific*.

Spec Homes

A spec home (speculative home for sale) is simply a tract home that is being built without anyone particular in mind. Spec homes are also known as inventory homes. Builders like to have a few homes ready, or almost ready, for buyers who need to move quickly. Sometimes a spec home is available because the original buyer backed out of the transaction for some reason. The same pros and cons that exist for tract homes are true for spec homes. You can usually negotiate a far better deal on a spec home than on a build job.

Buying a Tract or Spec Home

Buying a new tract or spec home is *much* different than buying a resale home, and you will find your Realtor to be an invaluable asset throughout the process, for the reasons discussed here.

Most builders use their own contract rather than the contract promulgated by the real estate commission, and the contract was *not* written to be fair.

The contract was written to benefit the builder, not you.

And, although it varies by area, most of the salespeople at a builder's model are not Realtors; they work for the builder and are not licensed or regulated by the state. That means that they don't have a legal requirement to treat you fairly and the only knowledge they have about construction and real estate is what they learn in their training classes. Some builder representatives are better than others, of course. There are some who know a great deal about construction and others that know much about interior design.

The one thing they all have in common, however, is that they want you to buy a house. They really don't care if you like the house, as long as you close and don't say mean things about them online.

Builders welcome, *and usually prefer,* buyers who are represented by Realtors. Does it cost you more to use a Realtor? Sometimes. Most builders say that Realtor commissions come out of their marketing budget so the buyer is not really paying commissions, and I am sure that's true some of the time. Generally, when builders are selling spec homes, they ask the potential buyer if they have a Realtor before they quote them their best price. That price might be higher if there is a Realtor involved. But don't assume that any extra money is going in your pocket if you choose to not have a Realtor represent you. It's probably not. The builder might make it look like a good deal on the front end, but they'll make it up on the back end, and you'll never know the difference.

> *Do not begrudge a Realtor the fee they are paid for their expertise; they are there to keep you from getting ripped off.*

If you didn't have a Realtor, you would have to pay a lawyer, and lawyers don't know very much about buying a home, beyond the contracts and title work. If you plan to have your Realtor represent you in the purchase of a new home, be sure you mention to the salesperson that you have representation on your first visit (if your agent isn't with you). Or, better yet, give the builder your Realtor's card and tell him to contact them, instead of you, with information. It will send a signal that they are not going to be able to rip you off, and it will guarantee that the builder works with your Realtor, since some builders require that your agent be announced on your first visit to their model.

What You Need to Know About New Construction

Spec homes are often listed on the MLS, so your Realtor can show them to you just like any other MLS listed home. If you visit the model on your own, the onsite salesperson can show you a list of their homes that are available immediately or within a month or two. Here are some things you should know about buying a spec or building a tract home:

- Builders are most anxious to sell their spec homes first, and here's why. The interest rate for homes under construction (construction financing) is far lower than the rate for homes that are finished and move-in ready. It is expensive for builders to keep homes in inventory; so spec homes are generally far more negotiable than build jobs, especially if you can close quickly.

- Builders do not like to reduce their prices and risk upsetting other buyers who might have paid more. You can generally expect a small reduction in price (if any) but a larger number of "free" upgrades like tile or granite.

- The home you buy will look nothing like the model. Builders use higher quality materials in their models, and their models are staged to attract buyers. In fact, there is an entire industry dedicated to the cause. I suggest you do not even walk through the model, unless you are just looking for decorating ideas. Look at one of their spec homes or a build job that is near completion. Do not be fooled by smoke and mirrors.

- You still need an inspection on a new home. In fact, you need it more since you will be the first person to live in the house.

- If you are building a home, the salesperson will want to write the contract to reflect a sales price plus a detailed list of upgrades, and you are expected to decide what you want before you even go to the design center. A better way is to negotiate a dollar amount or a budget to use at the design center.

- When building, be sure to insist on an inspection before the sheetrock goes up to ensure that the space between the studs is clean. It is not uncommon for workers to leave trash and food in the empty house and for garbage and sawdust to be left in between the walls.

- Do not ever, ever, ever buy a home from a builder before re-searching their reputation online. And do not be afraid to talk to neighbors and find out about their experience.

- Although new homes come with all kinds of warranties, do not assume the builder is going to honor them, even when they use a third-party warranty company. Warranty companies go out of business all the time, and they have all kinds of "out" clauses that they can use to get out of fixing your house. It is best to pretend that you are buying a resale home, and hope you get lucky when you file a warranty claim.

- Builders have preferred lenders or may even own their own mort-gage companies and title companies. They will often offer you $5,000 in closing costs, for example, if you use their lender. They will claim that their rates are competitive, but you *must* shop around and do your due diligence. Builders will say they prefer their own lenders because they can control the loan process, but that isn't true. Owning a mortgage company is another profit cen-ter for the builders. As a buyer, it's all about the math. The cheapest loan, after factoring in the builder's contribution to your closing costs, gets your business. Cost means total cost, not up-front cost. You are losing money if the builder gives you $5,000 in closing costs but offers you a 4.5 percent interest rate, when you can get 4.25 percent or less through another mortgage com-pany. In the long run, you will save a lot more than $5,000 when you get a loan with a lower interest rate. Do not be held hostage by $5,000 and the games builders play. Many of my buyers find it is cheaper to use their own lender.

- Builders also offer incentives to use their title company, if they are affiliated with one. The incentive is that they will pay for your title policy. If the title incentive is separate from the mortgage incentive, it can be a pretty good deal. If not, it is, once again, all about the math.

I understand the allure of buying a brand new home. Have a good agent represent you, but do your research, do the math, and hope for the best.

Foreclosures and Short Sales

When a homeowner stops making his or her mortgage payment, the bank takes back the house in a process called foreclosure. A short sale is a house that sells for less than the balance on its mortgage. Banks must approve short sales, and it is typically in their best interest to do so since they will recoup more money than they would if the house went into foreclosure.

The techniques used to buy a property that has been foreclosed upon, and the risks involved in doing so, are beyond the scope of this book. My experience with foreclosures has demonstrated to me that it is difficult to make the math work. Let's say there is a bank-owned property (foreclosure) that interests you, and that the sales price is $200,000. You estimate that the home needs roughly $35,000 worth of repairs and improvements. Your Realtor analyzes the market for you and determines that homes of similar size in good condition sell for an average of $245,000. Assuming you do not have any unexpected surprises, you fix up the house and make a $10,000 profit. Is $10,000 enough to justify the substantial risk and effort involved with buying properties that are typically in poor condition? To some, it is. It was to me when I first started flipping homes. I soon realized I was making below minimum wage for my efforts and learned that I had to start buying homes a lot cheaper if I was going to make a living as a flipper.

It is very difficult, in my opinion and in this market, to buy a foreclosed house cheap enough to make it worth the trouble and to justify the risk. The only exception I have found involves very high-end luxury homes costing over a million dollars. So, if you are in the market for a multi-million dollar home, you should keep your eyes open for a good foreclosure. Otherwise - buyer beware.

Short sales can be worth pursuing under certain circumstances. The problem, however, is that the bank can takes several weeks, or even months, to approve the contract. It can take a year to close. If you are looking at short sales, focus on the ones that already have bank approval, and save yourself months of not knowing if you are going to be able to buy a particular house. It's just not smart to tie your money up that way.

Buying a home without a Realtor

If you have found a home or have a relationship with someone selling his or her home, you can hire a Realtor or real estate consultant to manage the transaction for you. The Realtor would be a neutral third-party participant to the transaction who would write the offers and amendments, manage inspections, and guide both the seller and buyer through the closing. The cost is generally split between the buyer and the seller. You may have to find an independent agent since many of the larger real estate brokerages will not work this way.

{ 3 }

House Hunting

Once you know what you want to buy, where you want to buy it, and how much you can pay for it, it's time to go house hunting. I've found that a methodical approach is best, as discussed in the following section.

Get the Dogs Out

Go through the list you received from your Realtor and get rid of the "dogs." Dogs are homes that have structural problems, are bordered by power lines or commercial property, or are obviously dumps, unless you are looking for a fixer upper, of course. You can generally eliminate many homes just by looking at the pictures and reading the description. If you received an electronic list, you will be able to view many pictures of each home and even take virtual tours.

If you want a home in pristine condition, get rid of anything that says, "handyman special" or "bring your decorating ideas." If you want to rehab a home, get rid of homes that say, "Mrs. Clean lives here" or "Pristine!"

Do not eliminate too many homes based strictly on the exterior; the interior may be spectacular and worth a look.

Landscaping is easy to fix. Your goal is to get rid of the homes that obviously will not work for you. The ones that make the first cut are now "Possibilities."

Narrowing Down the Possibilities

Possibilities are homes worth further exploration. Start narrowing down your Possibilities list by going to Google Maps to see what surrounds the house, if it wasn't obvious from the picture. If you notice that the back of the property is bordered by power lines, commercial property, busy streets, or railroad tracks, move it to the "Reject" pile. Quite often you can view surveys, disclosures, floorplans, and other potentially relevant information.

As you go through your list, you'll find homes that really excite you and others about which you are uncertain. Move the ones that excite you to your "Favorites" pile and leave the rest in "Possibilities." Send both lists to your agent, and schedule some time to visit your Favorites. Once your agent has a good idea what you like, he or she can explore your "Possibilities" list for you and take you to see ones that might work. Your agent will learn a lot about you based on the homes you chose.

Viewing Homes

On your first visit to a home, see if you like the way it feels before you spend too much time there. If the condition of the home activates your gag reflex, move on. You will be surprised by how many homes that look beautiful from the outside or in the pictures are actually dogs on the inside. You will not hurt your agent's feelings if you don't like the house, and there is no point in wasting time in a house that you hate. If you find that you like the way the house feels, analyze the floor plan and try to envision how you would live there. As you are walking through, make mental notes about the general condition of the house. Keep your eyes open for cracks in the walls, slanted floors, water damage, mold, and other troublesome areas. Listed here are some other things to consider when viewing a house.

Floor Plans

The flow of the house needs to make sense. You need the right number of rooms and a place for everyone in the family to work, play, and sleep. Because people live differently, floor plans are not "one size fits all." Here are some general rules that apply to most people:

Formal Living & Dining – Combo

I usually try to steer buyers away from the "combo" or stacked plan (Figure 1). In a combo plan, the formal living room and formal dining room are one large space, which takes up much of the front of the house. Most people don't want formal living spaces anymore, favoring home office space instead. In a combo plan, there is a lot of wasted space. Look for split formals rather than stacked formals, discussed next.

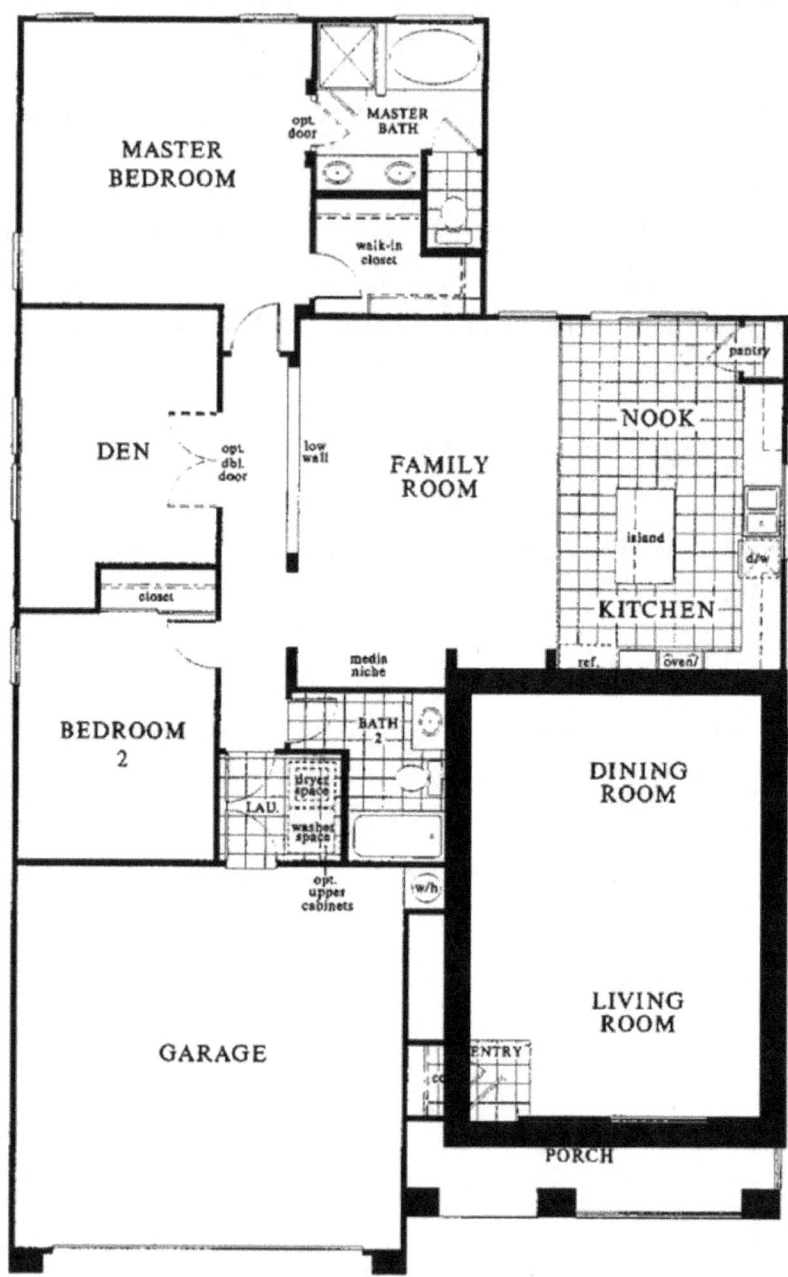

Figure 1: Living Room/Dining Room - Combo

Formal Living & Dining – Split

A split formal floor plan (Figure 2) has the dining room on one side of the front door and the formal living room on the other. Adding French doors to the formal living room will transform it into a home office.

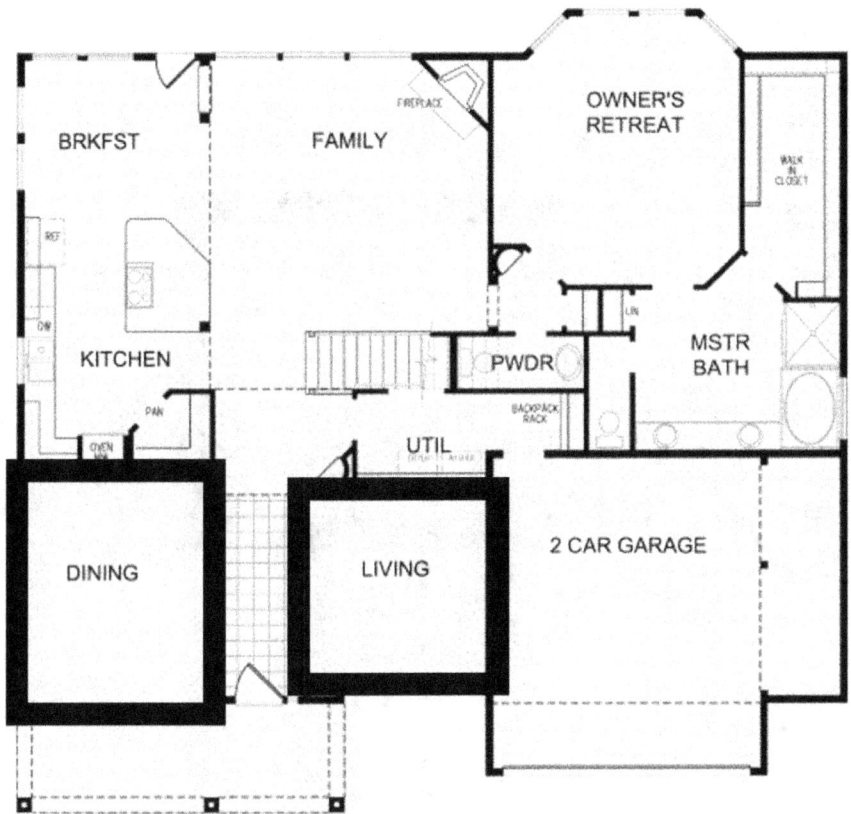

Figure 2: Split Formals

Open Concept Kitchen/Family Room

An open concept kitchen (Figure 3) is one in which the kitchen, breakfast room, and family room exist as one large space rather than smaller sectioned areas. Generally speaking, this type of space is very, very popular.

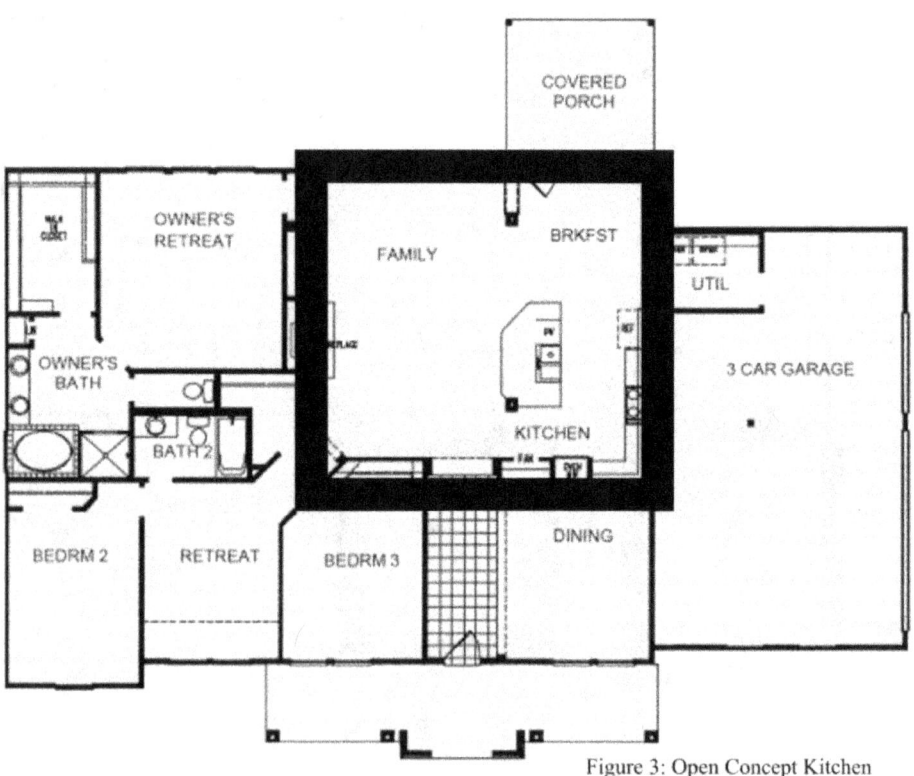

Figure 3: Open Concept Kitchen

Master Bedroom

A large percentage of newer homes have the master bedroom on the first floor. The perceived benefit is that the adults are downstairs and the kids are upstairs, so the downstairs area stays neater and quieter. Some buyers have learned the hard way that it is extremely inconvenient to have a new baby in a nursery on the second floor, away from Mom and Dad. The choice is yours. Today's buyers still favor a downstairs master, even knowing that the crib and changing table may end up in a corner in the master bedroom, at least for a while.

Be mindful of the location of the downstairs master bedroom. The location preferred by most is in the back of the house, but there should be at least a small hallway to separate the master bedroom from the family room (Figure 4). In other words, you should not be able to look into the master bedroom from the family room.

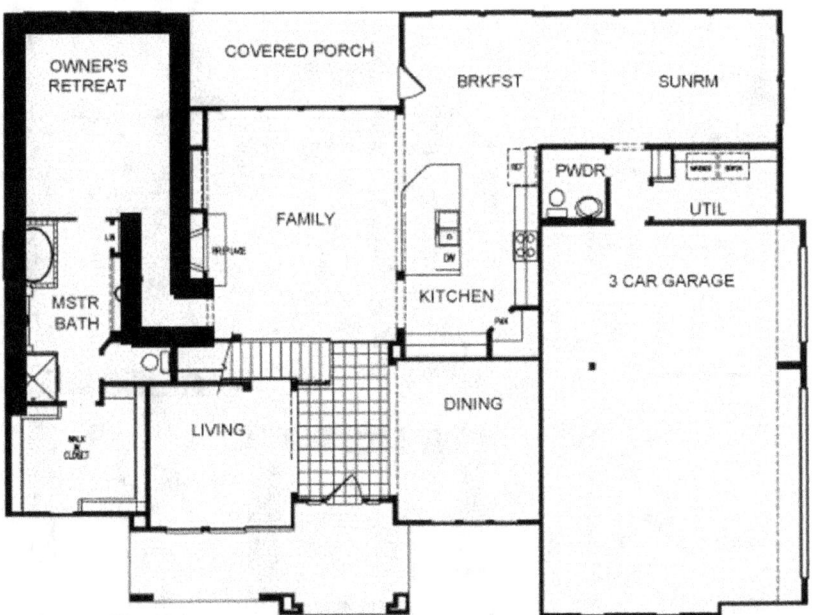

Figure 4: Master down with separation from family room

Master bedrooms located in the front of the house are not nearly as desirable as ones located in the back (Figure 5). Though not necessarily a deal killer, you will lose buyers when it is time to resell the home. An ideal and highly sought after floor plan is one with both the master and a second bedroom downstairs, and two or three bedrooms upstairs, as pictured next.

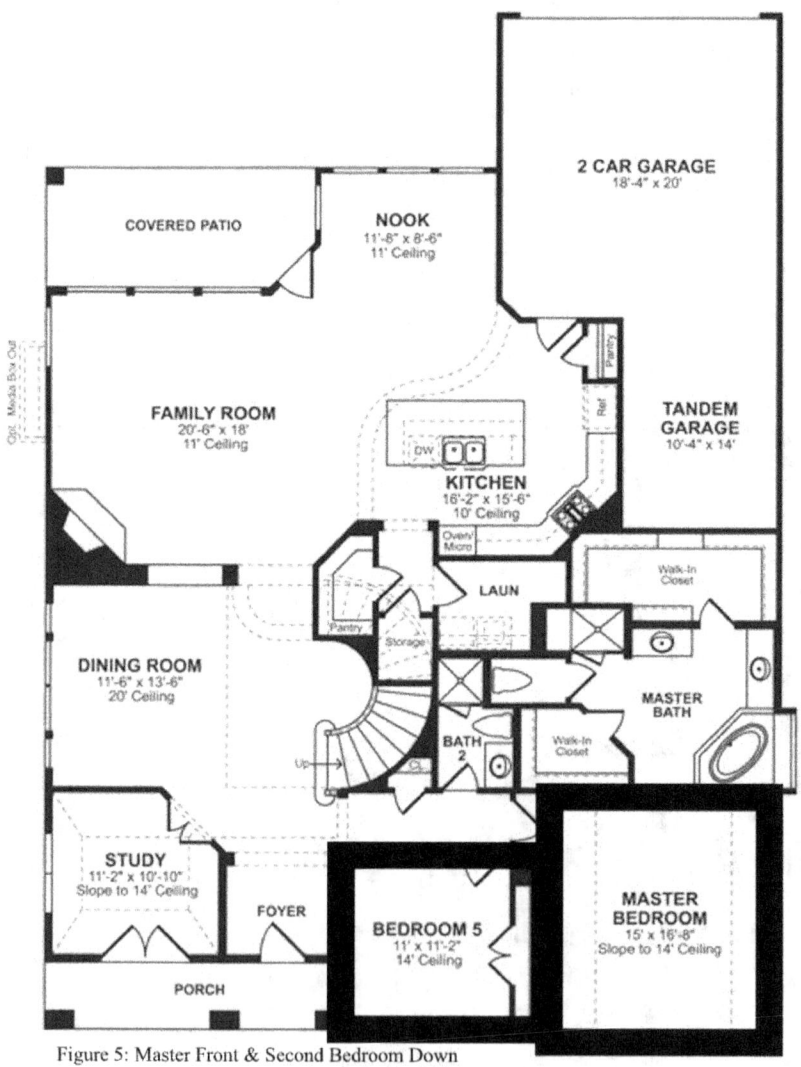

Figure 5: Master Front & Second Bedroom Down

Kitchen

An ideal floor plan is one in which the garage opens into the utility room, which leads to the kitchen, so you do not have to carry your groceries from the garage across the house to the kitchen (Figure 6). Also illustrated in this example is the odd location of the utility room, next to the formal living spaces.

Figure 6: Garage/Kitchen Split

Split Bedrooms

In single-story homes, homes with a three-way split allow family members some privacy. As can be seen in Figure 7, bedrooms are located on opposite sides of the home, separated by the family room.

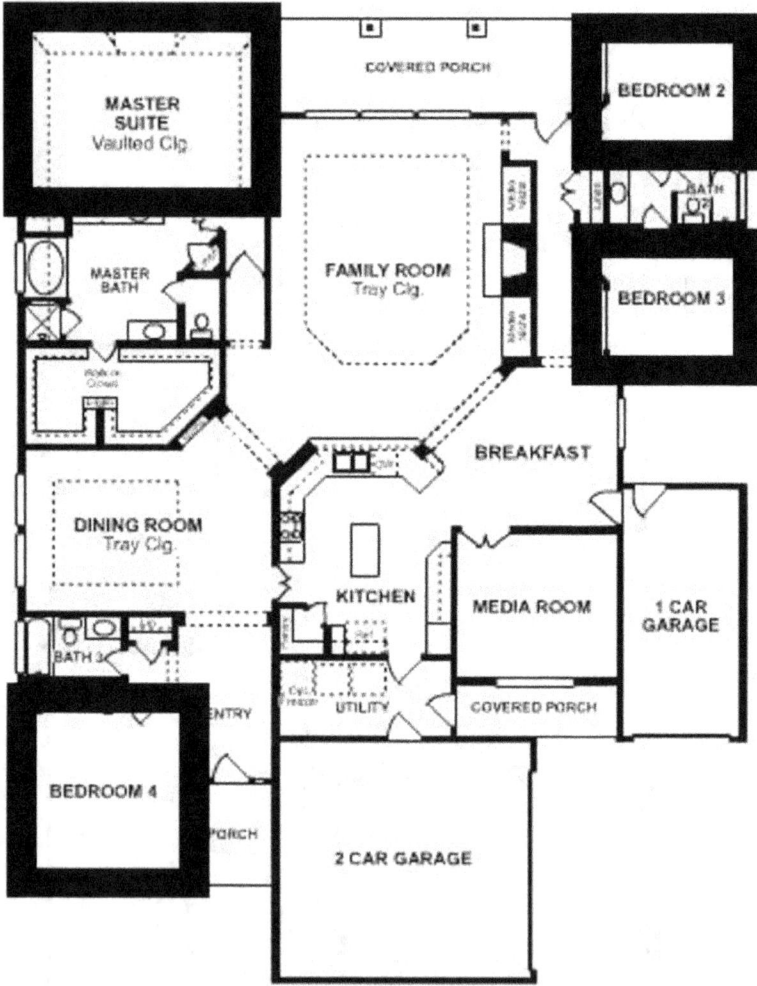

Figure 7: Split Bedrooms

Resale

The secret to buying a home with good resale potential is to buy one that will attract the largest pool of buyers. *Stated differently, don't buy a home that has a feature that no one in their right mind would want!* That means none of the following: homes in bad locations, such as next to busy streets, schools, commercial property, or power lines; homes without a garage, pantry, or linen closet; homes that have the smallest yard in the neighborhood; and homes with small closets and inadequate storage. The owners of these types of homes will try to distract you with beautiful landscaping, hardwood floors, and stainless steel appliances. Don't be the buyer of someone else's problem. Just don't!

Property Condition

If you are working with an exclusive buyer agent, he or she will undoubtedly be able to help you spot obvious flaws in the condition of the home and will recognize unpopular floor plans. Realtors are not inspectors, but you should be able to rely on them to point out obvious issues like roof and foundation problems. My personal guarantee to my buyer/clients is that if the inspection uncovers something that leads them to walk away from the house, I will pay for their next inspection.

> *It's not unreasonable to expect the agent you hire to have the same level of knowledge and confidence in their skill set.*

The seller is required to disclose everything to you that he knows to be wrong with the property. Between your agent and the seller, you should have a pretty good idea of the condition of the property before you hire an inspector. The following includes some general guidelines on what to look for when evaluating a property. Note that different materials are used in different parts of the country, and this list is not meant to be all-inclusive.

Roof

If the roof is more than 15-20 years old, chances are it needs to be replaced. But younger roofs can also fail. Look for shingles that are lifting up, cracked, have curled edges, or are even missing altogether, and take note of areas where the granules have worn off. Also look for water stains on the underside of the roof and on the ceiling.

Foundation

Foundation problems are usually caused by bad drainage, ground movement, or poor construction, which causes the foundation to shift or settle. Signs of foundation problems include doors and windows that no longer open or close, drywall cracks, and cracks in the bricks. Less obvious clues are cracks in the slab that can sometimes be seen on vinyl floors, cracked tiles that do not lay flat, and a slanted floor.

Sprinkler

It is very common for sprinkler heads to break, usually when someone runs over them with the lawn mower. The control box located in the garage turns the system on and off, and is usually zoned for front, back, and sides. Be certain you know what you are buying. Some homes only have sprinklers installed in the front or back. You do not want to overpay for the home because you have assumed the yard is fully sprinklered.

Air Conditioners and Heaters

Your inspector will test the heater and air conditioner to verify their operability, but it is important that you get an idea of their age and general condition before you make an offer. Take a look at both the inside and outside units, and take note of dust and rust in the vents. Improper maintenance will significantly shorten the life of heating and cooling systems. If the units are very old or seem to be neglected, be sure to factor the replacement cost into your offer.

Windows

When air gets between the two pieces of glass in a double pane window, the condensation can cause foggy windows. The only fix for this is to replace the glass. Your inspector will check each and every window, but try to get a general idea of their condition before you make an offer. If the house needs all new windows, the cost will run into the thousands.

Plumbing

Your inspector will check the plumbing system, but take note of leaking faucets, showerheads, and toilets, and also ascertain the age of the water heater by looking at the label on the unit. If the water heater is old and located in the attic, you will want it replaced since a leak will damage the inside of the house. If it is located in the garage, all gas and some electric water heaters must be on a stand eighteen inches off the floor and they must have an expansion tank. Straps are required in earthquake zones.

Exposure

The direction a house faces is called its "exposure" and is a matter of personal preference. In some cultures, an east-facing home is considered lucky and the buyer will not consider any other exposure. If the front of a house faces north, the back yard has more sun in the summer. Homes facing south generally have shade in the backyard in the afternoon, which is desirable in warmer climates. The floor plan and location of the rooms will determine the comfort level of the home.

Pests

Your lender may require a certificate from your inspector stating that the home is free of termites and other critters. Even if it is not a lender requirement, you will definitely want to know if the home has an active termite infestation or has been treated in the past. If prior treatments to the property have occurred, find out if they were partial treatments or if the whole house was treated. Sometimes, if only one side of the house is treated, the termites will simply move from one side of the house to the other.

Lead-Based Paint

Homes built before 1978 usually have been painted with lead-based paint. The seller or their agent is required to give you the EPA booklet titled "Protect Your Family From Lead in Your Home."

The seller must disclose any known lead-based paint hazards and give you any relevant records. The risk with lead-based paint is when children or pets ingest it, since the lead can cause brain damage. Typically homes that originally had lead-based paint have been repainted many times through the years, and this reduces the risks substantially.

Environmental Hazards

Sellers are also required to disclose any known environmental hazards like leaking underground oil tanks, the presence of asbestos, and lead pipes, among others. There can be serious health and financial consequences associated with the remediation of these hazards; know what you are buying and what risks you are assuming.

Floodplains

You need to know if the home is located in a floodplain. If it is, your lender is going to require flood insurance. The extra expense may or may not be a deal breaker, but you are entitled to know your risks and responsibilities before you sign your name on the dotted line. You can go to http://www.floodsmart.gov/floodsmart/ to review the flood maps in your area.

Nuisance Factors

When you are at the house, listen for things that can make you crazy, like barking dogs, traffic from local schools or restaurants, airplanes, trains, and noise from distant freeways. Remember, even if it doesn't bother you during the day, the noise may annoy you at night.

Narrowing It Down

The truth is that the perfect house doesn't exist. Even people who build a custom home find things they wish they had designed differently. With any luck, you will find yourself with a short list of two or three homes. So, how do you decide which home to buy? The secret to buying a home without losing your shirt is to first use your head, then your heart.

As they did in the old days, get out your yellow legal pad. First, draw a line down the middle of the page and write the positive aspects of your prospective house on one side and the negative aspects on the other; each finalist gets their own page. Hopefully, you have already eliminated homes in bad locations, with bad foundations and undesirable floor plans, and you are left with homes that are perfectly safe investments with good potential for resale. Rank your choices, and compare and contrast the top two.

The Top Two

You still need more information about your top choices. Ask your agent to send you the following documents on each home, although if he or she is a good agent, you won't have to ask:

Comparable Marketing Analysis (CMA)

Your agent will research information about comparable properties in the area using the MLS, including active listings, pending sales, and expired listings. After making adjustments for property condition and other factors, he or she will recommend a sales price for the home. Do not be surprised if a price range is recommended, rather than a firm price. By reviewing the CMA, you will know immediately if the house is priced too high or too low.

> *It is very easy for your Realtor to manipulate the numbers to make it appear that a home is worth more or less than is actually the case. Ask your agent to send you all the raw data that they used in their report, including active listings, expired listings, sold listings, and listings that are sold but haven't closed yet. Hopefully they don't "accidently on purpose" forget to send you a listing that would have a major impact on the pricing of the home.*

Price/Square Foot

Larger homes are priced lower per square foot, and smaller homes are priced higher per square foot. Why? The value of the land has to be concentrated into the price of the home. The smaller the home, the more the value is concentrated.

It is not helpful to take an average of the price per square foot of homes in the neighborhood and multiply it by the square footage to come up with an offer. However, the information is useful in tracking trends and ensuring that the home is priced comparably to other homes of the same size and condition.

Seller's Disclosure Report

Sellers are required by law to disclose everything that they know about the property. In Texas, they do so on a form promulgated by the Texas Real Estate Commission called the Seller's Disclosure Report. From this report you will learn the age and condition of all of the components in the house.

Review this report very carefully and remember that the accuracy of these reports is contingent upon the seller's knowledge of the property and his or her integrity.

Some sellers lie in order to present their home in the best possible light! That's why you need an inspection.

Tax Rolls

You or your agent can go online to the county tax assessor's website and uncover all types of information about the property. While you are investigating, try to uncover the following:

Discrepancies in Square Footage

The square footage listed in the tax rolls can be substantially different than the square footage the seller claims. A 100 square foot variance at $90/square foot is $9,000! Know what you're buying.

Tax Assessed Value (TAV)

The TAV is *not* the same thing as market value; do not assume for a second that the TAV is the price you should pay for the house. You pay property taxes based on the TAV, and this figure is typically lower than market value. If this figure is higher than what your agent told you the house was worth, investigate why this may be the case. Also look to see if the TAV has been increased or decreased each year. If it is consistently on a downward trend, then you may be in an area with depreciating values. Why are prices dropping? It could be that the area was overvalued in the first place, but you need to know for sure. Or, it could just be indicative of the real estate market in general.

Neighborhood Demographics and Factoids

Most agents have access to this type of information and can present it to you in a pretty little package. You do not have to guess who your neighbors are; the information is out there for free! Use this information like pieces of a puzzle to learn everything you can about the property and area before you write an offer and spend any money.

History Report

It's not hard to learn the history of the property. On the tax assessor's website you should be able to learn when the seller purchased the house, from whom, and how many other previous owners there were. You can sometimes find out how much the seller paid and the amount of his or her original loan. It helps to know how much equity a homeowner has, if you can figure it out. If, for example, the seller owes more than what the house is worth at today's prices, the seller is "upside down" and will need to bring money to the closing table. You need to make sure that they have the cash to sell the house. If not, you're dealing with a short sale transaction, which was discussed earlier.

{ 4 }

Offers & Negotiations

For some, negotiating the deal is the most stressful part of the homebuying process. How much should we offer? What if it's too high? What if it's too low? Are there any other offers? Is this the right house?

These questions and others cause buyers a lot of sleepless nights. Me? I love to negotiate the price and terms of a transaction. I love the strategizing, the opportunity to outsmart the competition, and the thrill of getting my client a home they love at a good price. The sections that follow discuss the process in detail.

Making an Offer

This is when the gamesmanship starts, and this is why you need a strong negotiator to represent you. Before you make an offer, have your agent call the seller's agent to see if they have any offers or contracts. You do not want to lose your second choice home if your first choice is sold. This call is an opportunity for your agent to learn why the seller is moving and how desperate he or she is to sell the home. If the listing agent is practically begging for an offer, you can submit a lower offer.

The seller might be in the midst of negotiating a contract with another buyer. If they have verbalized a deal and are just waiting for signatures, it is time to move on. Or, if you really love the house, you can still submit an offer and the seller's agent will be required to present it to the seller/client (unless the seller instructed the agent not to present any more offers). If nothing else, your contract can be in a backup position.

The seller's agent will undoubtedly tell your agent to submit your best offer to try to knock out the first buyer. In very competitive markets, you really may have to submit your best price, but in my area I typically advise my clients not to play that game. I prefer to submit roughly the same offer I would otherwise, but really sell my client's credentials and commitment to close. I also encourage my buyers to accommodate the seller's closing time frame, if at all possible. Your first goal should be to beat out the other buyer and next to negotiate the price and terms. Being flexible in your closing date can help you accomplish this.

Sometimes the seller's agent will state that they are expecting an offer on the property "any minute" and will encourage you to submit an offer ASAP. Or, he or she will tell you how many people have expressed an interest in the house and will try to convince you that the home is going to sell very quickly. These are obvious sales tactics used to generate an offer on the property.

Your agent cannot know for sure if the other agent is being truthful or if they are just playing games.

Take a look at how long the home has been on the market. If it is a new listing and it is a great house, the agent might be telling the truth. If it has been on the market for over a month or two, there probably is no bidding war, and the agent is probably playing games.

Initial Offer

Based on everything you have learned while researching the property, you need to come up with your initial offer. This amount will be based on the property condition, days on market, the CMA that your agent produced, and what you perceive as the seller's determination to sell the home. I use the word "perceived" because you never really know what the seller's situation might be.

As discussed in the next section, price is not the only negotiable item to include when you write an offer. If you know that you are going to ask for a carpet allowance, include that in your initial offer. If you know of certain repairs that you require, ask for them up front. You can be specific about the closing date or leave it blank and let the seller choose the date. Your agent will generate the paperwork and present it to you for your review and signature. After getting your signature and any required deposits, they will present the offer to the seller's agent, who will then present it to the seller.

Other Points of Negotiation

There are other issues besides price that warrant tough negotiations. The following section discusses these issues.

Possession

A seller vacating the property and a buyer taking possession is the source of many potential conflicts. The sellers do not want to leave the home until they are absolutely certain that the transaction has closed, and buyers are not always comfortable with sellers living in homes that they just purchased. What if they won't leave?

In Texas, it's common for the seller to be given 48 hours to vacate the property after closing. If the property happens to be vacant, the buyers can usually take possession right after funding.

The terms of possession must be agreed upon before you execute your purchase offer, and the specifics must be committed to in writing!

You should never, ever, ever let the sellers stay in the home after closing without a signed Temporary Lease Agreement.

If they refuse to vacate the property, you will need a lease to evict them. If you don't utilize a lease agreement, you will be required to go to court for the eviction. Be sure to include in your lease a holdover fee, so if the seller doesn't move out on time, you are compensated.

If the seller is only going to be leasing the property for 48 hours, I generally don't request a deposit or rent. It's a goodwill gesture. I hope that if my buyer makes it easy for them to move, they will reciprocate by taking good care of the property and cleaning the house on their way out. If the seller is going to stay any longer than that, I ask the title company to hold back a few hundred dollars from the seller's proceeds in case the property is damaged. If they leave without incident, the money is promptly returned.

Earnest Money

The purpose of earnest money is to show that you are sincere about purchasing the property. In a hot seller's market, you may have to put up more earnest money to appear more interested in the house than a competing buyer. In slow markets or with desperate, motivated sellers, you can get away with less. As long as you abide by the terms of the contract, you get your money back at closing as a credit against your closing costs or down payment. Your Realtor should have contingencies in your contract (discussed earlier) to protect your earnest money in case the house does not appraise, your financing falls through, or if the house is uninsurable.

Closing Date

Accommodating the seller with respect to the closing date is an easy way to steal a house from another buyer. Selling a home can be as stressful as buying one! The seller might be under contract to purchase a different home, but they usually can't qualify for their new mortgage until their current home has sold and closed. In addition, they don't want to vacate their property until after closing since they don't want two housing payments. All of their plans are contingent upon the buyer. Anything a buyer can do to make it easier on the seller is going to mean more to the seller than cash.

If a house is vacant, the seller will be very happy with a quick closing. In my area, a quick closing is three weeks. If you can close quickly, the seller will often sell for less since they won't have to make their next month's mortgage payment on an empty home. If the home is still occupied, the seller may not have any place to go. Working around their schedule and making their move as easy on them as possible can save you thousands. If it turns out that you can't accommodate their needs, you're a nice guy for making the offer.

Closing Costs

When a seller pays your closing costs, the benefit for you is that it takes less cash to buy the house. Technically, you're not really saving the money; the closing costs get rolled into your mortgage. But it does make purchasing a home doable for qualified buyers that are short on cash.

Sellers will never have a problem paying your closing costs because they are only concerned about their net, or the amount of the money that goes in their pocket after closing. Let's look at an example. The following two offers are the same to the seller:

Offer One		Offer Two	
Sales Price:	$205,000	Sales Price:	$200,000
Seller paid closing costs:	$ 5,000	Seller paid closing costs:	$ 0,000
Seller's net proceeds	$200,000	Seller's net proceeds	$200,000

Lenders restrict the amount of the seller's contribution, usually to 3% of the sales price. Check with your lender regarding any limits or restrictions specific to your chosen financing.

Competing Offers

If you believe that there truly is a competing buyer for a house that you want, have your agent call the seller's agent and let him know you are writing an offer, and ask him to see what they can learn about the seller's situation. Are they relocating? Have they found another place to live? How quickly do they need to move?

Do not assume that you need to pay more to beat out the other guy. If you can be flexible with your closing date, it is often more important to the seller than the cash. It is extremely stressful to sell a house. If you can accommodate the seller's needs, it will go a long way in helping you win the offer war.

Negotiating Strategies

After your offer is presented to the seller, he or she has the option to accept your offer, reject your offer, or make a counteroffer. Remember that everything is negotiable, not just the price. In my twenty years in the industry, I have noticed a few patterns in the way sellers respond to the offers I submit on behalf of my buyer/clients. They include:

The Cave

The Seller accepts the offer with no changes. They agree to the price, closing date, home warranty, title policy, closing costs, etc. This only happens with the most desperate sellers, typically ones who are in danger of losing the home. On deals like these, the seller usually has little or no money to make repairs, so be prepared to buy the house "as is."

Seller comes down in price by $1000

This means that they think your initial offer is ridiculous but they do want to try to work with you. It is an invitation for you to submit a better offer. This type of response upsets some buyers, which I don't understand. The initial offer gives a lot of information about the seller's circumstances and level of motivation: it means they are not desperate and are not going to give the house away.

Baby Steps

Here, the seller responds to your offer by dropping $3,000-$4,000. As a buyer, you respond by coming up $3,000-$4000, and so forth. The parties go back and forth until one or the other claims it is his or her final offer, usually after the third round.

Split the difference

Some sellers hate to negotiate and view it as confrontational. These people just want to split the difference and get it over with. I've found that it is usually quite easy to get the seller to reduce their asking price a little more in this scenario, if not with price, then with other negotiable items like repairs.

What Not to Do

Some buyers are their own worst enemies. Here are some things buyers do during negotiations that cost them money.

They have a long list of complaints about the house.

Some inexperienced buyers like to present the seller with a long list of things that they think are wrong with the house in order to get a better price. This "I'm doing you a favor by buying your home" attitude does nothing but antagonize the seller and creates an unfriendly and risky transaction. If the buyer is making an offer to purchase a property, they clearly like the house and see value in owning it. If the seller has an opportunity to sell the home to someone more pleasant, they will. And if they don't, they are not going to care for and leave the house in good condition when they leave.

Play nice or pay a price.

They use their hearts, not their heads.

The homebuying process is tedious, stressful and, at times, exhausting. There are few decisions greater than this one! By the time you pick a house, you are going to be emotionally invested. This is where you really need a good agent to be your voice of reason. Control your emotions until after repairs have been negotiated and you are sure it is a good house.

They overpay because they are afraid of losing the house.

There are definitely times when you have to submit your best offer, but more often than not there is plenty of room for negotiation. Take an objective look at the seller's situation, the general real estate climate in your area, and the raw data that your agent provides to see how long it takes similar homes to sell. If the home has a unique feature that can't be found anywhere else, you may need to pay more. If you can find a home similar to this one on any given block, don't submit your best offer right away.

Counteroffers & Acceptance

Once you make your initial offer, the seller will respond as described above. You will know immediately which strategy the seller is using and you will know how to respond. I strongly recommend that you keep asking for discounts until the seller says "no" twice. If, for example, you have gone three rounds with the seller and they come back with their best and final offer, don't believe them. Make another counteroffer and see what happens. If they still say no, go ahead and accept.

Contingencies

A contingency in your contract will allow you to back out of the deal without penalty if anything goes wrong. Some Realtors will say that buyers use them because they are not sure that they want to buy the house. *These Realtors work for the seller.* As a buyer, you do not want to spend money inspecting and appraising a home if the seller is not legally obligated to sell you the home once you do. Writing a contract with contingencies allows you the time you need to do your due diligence. Here are some common contract contingencies:

Financing Contingency

A financing contingency says that your offer is contingent upon you being able to secure financing for the property within a certain period of time. It specifies in detail the type of financing, the terms, and how long you have to obtain loan approval. Unless you are buying a home with cash, you should always include a Financing Contingency. If your financing falls through, at least you'll get your deposit back.

Twenty days is usually plenty of time for you to secure financing. The deal does not have to close in twenty days, but you should have your loan approved with "conditions." Conditional loan approval means that the bank will lend you money once certain conditions are met, like the appraisal, job verification, a certain bank statement, and so forth.

Appraisal Contingency

The appraisal contingency has become an important one in some parts of the country where home prices have dropped significantly. The appraisal contingency says that if the house does not appraise for at least the purchase price, you can back out of the deal. You can also write it to say that if the house doesn't appraise for the purchase price, the seller has to drop the price; if they refuses to do so, you can back out of the deal without penalty. Truth be told, if the house does not appraise, the bank will not lend you the money you need to buy the house. You will either have to pay cash for the difference (don't do this!), the seller will have to drop the price, or you will have to walk away from the deal.

Contingency for Sale of Another Property

This contingency is for buyers who have to sell their current home before they can buy a new one. Basically, it allows the buyer the right to back out of the deal if he or she cannot sell their current home. Contracts can also be written with a "kick-out" clause, which allows the seller to "kick out" the original contract if they find a new buyer that can close right away.

Option Fee & Earnest Money

An option fee is money paid by a buyer to a seller for the option to terminate the sales contract. An option gives the buyer time to have the house inspected and negotiate repairs, while at the same time it restricts the seller from selling the house to someone else. Buyers can terminate the contract during the option period for any reason. I write my contracts so that the buyer loses their option fee if they terminate the contract, but they get the money back if they close the transaction. The amount of the option fee is generally between $50 and $500 in my area.

Option fee funds should not be confused with earnest money. Earnest money is a security deposit that demonstrates the buyer's commitment to purchasing the property and is a show of good faith. The amount of earnest money is negotiable. Generally, you want to keep the amount of earnest money to a minimum, but high enough that the seller takes your offer seriously. Earnest money is placed in a trust account, usually at the title company. Earnest money is applied to the buyer's down payment and closing costs. If there is a failure to close through no fault of the buyer, the seller usually signs an agreement to release the funds back to the buyer, and vice versa, if the seller fails to close. Disputes do arise, however, and that is when you really need to be able to rely on your agent to get your money back.

Seller Markets

A seller's market is one in which there are more buyers than sellers; buyers must compete for the relatively few number of homes that are for sale. Competing offers drive up prices and buyers often have to spend more to get what they want.

Buying a home in a seller's market can be a frustrating experience. With some sellers receiving 5-15 offers within a few days of listing their home, it's important to write a contract that appeals to the seller, while at the same time makes sense for you. It's not uncommon for a buyer to become so anxious to win a bid that they throw common sense out the window.

Don't get so caught up in the game that you make poor decisions that can potentially cost you tens of thousands of dollars!

Contrary to what you have been told, it's not always a good time to buy a home. It's better to stay in an apartment for a few extra months than it is to overpay for a home or to assume a lot of financial risk.

The perfect contract – from a seller's perspective – would be all cash. The seller wouldn't have to pay for a title policy or make repairs, and the buyer would waive all their contingencies. The buyer's perspective is the exact opposite, of course. When buying a home in a seller's market, consider the following:

Price

Let's be honest – price trumps it all. Just as a buyer wants to pay as little as possible for a home, the seller wants to net as much as they possibly can. You sometimes need to make your first offer your best because you may not get a second chance.

Your lender isn't going to give you a blank check to buy anything that you want. The house needs to appraise for at least the sales price or you will have to figure out how to make up the difference.

Don't overpay for a home unless you are willing and able to pay the difference between the appraised value and the sales price in cash. If an appraiser states that a house is worth $100,000, would you be willing to pay $115,000 if that's the price you negotiated with the seller? If the answer is yes, ask yourself how long you plan to live in the home. It's going to take time to recoup the $15,000 you overpaid for the house.

Waiving Contingencies

Most sales contracts include clauses that allow the buyer to back out of the contract under certain circumstances and to get their down payment back. Sellers usually don't want to agree to these clauses because they don't want to risk tying up their property for several weeks or more, only to have the buyer walk away prior to closing. If you are waiving a financing contingency, be sure you qualify for your mortgage at interest rate and terms that are acceptable to you. If you are waiving an appraisal contingency, review the CMA provided by your agent to feel comfortable with the price you are paying. Have extra money in the bank if it doesn't appraise, or be prepared to walk away from the deal if the seller won't drop their price. If you are waiving your right to negotiate repairs, hire a great inspector and understand the property's condition and the level of risk you are assuming by doing so. Contingencies are discussed in greater detail later in this chapter.

Down Payment/Loan Terms

If a cash buyer is the perfect buyer, next best would be a buyer who has a large down payment (20% or more). Why? Simply put, a buyer who puts more money down has a better chance of closing the deal. Buyers who are strapped for cash may not have money to make lender-required repairs and probably won't have cash to close the deal if the house doesn't appraise. Low down payment loans weaken a buyer's position in a seller's market.

Seller-Paid Closing Costs

Sellers really only care about how much money they put in their pocket after a transaction closes. Rather than offering a higher sales price that might cause a problem with the appraisal, you can offer to pay some of the fees that sellers customarily pay at closing. The title policy, home warranty, real estate commission, legal fees, and transfer fees are all examples of seller-paid closing costs.

{ 5 }

Contracts

Texas Realtors use real estate contracts promulgated by the Texas Real Estate Commission. With the exception of the seller's listing agreement and the buyer's representation agreement, these documents were written to be fair to both the buyer and the seller, eliminating the need for most to hire an attorney. Your Realtor will simply fill in the blanks; no law school necessary.

There are dozens of contracts and addendums made available to Realtors. To review each document in detail is outside the scope of this book (not to mention really boring). The following sections will describe in detail those documents most commonly used in a Texas

Information About Brokerage Services

Every real estate agent in Texas is required to present you with the Information About Brokerage Services Form. They will ask you to sign it and will retain a copy for their records. This form is used to help explain the ways in which a real estate agent works, whom they represent, and what their basic duties are when representing parties in a real estate transaction. Signing this document obligates you to nothing. It's only an acknowledgement that you received the form. A sample Information About Brokerage Services form is pictured below:

Approved by the Texas Real Estate Commission for Voluntary Use   10-10-11

Texas law requires all real estate licensees to give the following information about brokerage services to prospective buyers, tenants, sellers and landlords.

Information About Brokerage Services

Before working with a real estate broker, you should know that the duties of a broker depend on whom the broker represents. If you are a prospective seller or landlord (owner) or a prospective buyer or tenant (buyer), you should know that the broker who lists the property for sale or lease is the owner's agent. A broker who acts as a subagent represents the owner in cooperation with the listing broker. A broker who acts as a buyer's agent represents the buyer. A broker may act as an intermediary between the parties if the parties consent in writing. A broker can assist you in locating a property, preparing a contract or lease, or obtaining financing without representing you. A broker is obligated by law to treat you honestly.

IF THE BROKER REPRESENTS THE OWNER:
The broker becomes the owner's agent by entering into an agreement with the owner, usually through a written - listing agreement, or by agreeing to act as a subagent by accepting an offer of subagency from the listing broker. A subagent may work in a different real estate office. A listing broker or subagent can assist the buyer but does not represent the buyer and must place the interests of the owner first. The buyer should not tell the owner's agent anything the buyer would not want the owner to know because an owner's agent must disclose to the owner any material information known to the agent.

IF THE BROKER REPRESENTS THE BUYER:
The broker becomes the buyer's agent by entering into an agreement to represent the buyer, usually through a written buyer representation agreement. A buyer's agent can assist the owner but does not represent the owner and must place the interests of the buyer first. The owner should not tell a buyer's agent anything the owner would not want the buyer to know because a buyer's agent must disclose to the buyer any material information known to the agent.

IF THE BROKER ACTS AS AN INTERMEDIARY:
A broker may act as an intermediary between the parties if the broker complies with The Texas Real Estate License Act. The broker must obtain the written consent of each party to the transaction to act as an intermediary. The written consent must state who will pay the broker and, in conspicuous bold or underlined print, set forth the broker's obligations as an intermediary. The broker is required to treat each party honestly and fairly and to comply with The Texas Real Estate License Act. A broker who acts as an intermediary in a transaction:

(1) shall treat all parties honestly;

(2) may not disclose that the owner will accept a price less than the asking price unless authorized in writing to do so by the owner;

(3) may not disclose that the buyer will pay a price greater than the price submitted in a written offer unless authorized in writing to do so by the buyer; and

(4) may not disclose any confidential information or any information that a party specifically instructs the broker in writing not to disclose unless authorized in writing to disclose the information or required to do so by The Texas Real Estate License Act or a court order or if the information materially relates to the condition of the property.

With the parties' consent, a broker acting as an intermediary between the parties may appoint a person who is licensed under The Texas Real Estate License Act and associated with the broker to communicate with and carry out instructions of one party and another person who is licensed under that Act and associated with the broker to communicate with and carry out instructions of the other party.

If you choose to have a broker represent you, you should enter into a written agreement with the broker that clearly establishes the broker's obligations and your obligations. The agreement should state how and by whom the broker will be paid. You have the right to choose the type of representation, if any, you wish to receive. Your payment of a fee to a broker does not necessarily establish that the broker represents you. If you have any questions regarding the duties and responsibilities of the broker, you should resolve those questions before proceeding.

Real estate licensee asks that you acknowledge receipt of this information about brokerage services for the licensee's records.

_____   _____
Buyer, Seller, Landlord or Tenant   Date
Mr. Seller, Mrs. Seller

One to Four Family Residential Contract (Resale)

The One to Four Family Residential Contract (Resale) is used for nearly all residential purchase transactions. The following images depict and describe the most commonly used terms and conditions from the perspective of the buyer.

1. Parties

Legal names should be used by all parties to the transaction. Buyers who will not be applying for financing do not need to be named here.

> 1. **PARTIES:** The parties to this contract are _____ Mr. Seller, Mrs. Seller _____
> (Seller) and _____ Mr. Buyer, Mrs. Buyer _____ (Buyer).
> Seller agrees to sell and convey to Buyer and Buyer agrees to buy from Seller the Property defined below.

2. Property

This section states the legal description of the property and lists the items that are included in the sale. Any item that is permanently attached to the property is included. Items that can easily be picked up and moved (like the washer/dryer or refrigerator) do not convey unless they become part of the negotiation process or the seller has specifically indicated that they are included in the sale. Most lenders now require that these items be listed on the 'Non-Realty Items Addendum' form rather than within the main contract. Accessories are items that are not necessarily attached to the property, but are still sold with the house. Pool equipment is an example of a home accessory that remains with the property. Items that the seller has specifically excluded from the transaction are listed in Section D. It's not uncommon, for example, for a seller to keep curtains that match their bedspread.

2. **PROPERTY:** The land, improvements and accessories are collectively referred to as the "Property".
  A. LAND: Lot _____3_____ Block _____D_____ , _____Villages of Coppell_____
  Addition, City of _____Coppell_____ , County of _____Dallas_____ ,
  Texas, known as _____123 Main Street_____ 75019
  (address/zip code), or as described on attached exhibit.
  B. IMPROVEMENTS: The house, garage and all other fixtures and improvements attached to the above-described real property, including without limitation, the following **permanently installed and built-in items,** if any: all equipment and appliances, valances, screens, shutters, awnings, wall-to-wall carpeting, mirrors, ceiling fans, attic fans, mail boxes, television antennas, mounts and brackets for televisions and speakers, heating and air-conditioning units, security and fire detection equipment, wiring, plumbing and lighting fixtures, chandeliers, water softener system, kitchen equipment, garage door openers, cleaning equipment, shrubbery, landscaping, outdoor cooking equipment, and all other property owned by Seller and attached to the above described real property.
  C. ACCESSORIES: The following described related accessories, if any: window air conditioning units, stove, fireplace screens, curtains and rods, blinds, window shades, draperies and rods, door keys, mailbox keys, above ground pool, swimming pool equipment and maintenance accessories, artificial fireplace logs, and controls for: (i) garage doors, (ii) entry gates, and (iii) other improvements and accessories.
  D. EXCLUSIONS: The following improvements and accessories will be retained by Seller and must be removed prior to delivery of possession: <u>drapes in the master bedroom.</u>

3. Sales Price

Line A is the buyer's down payment, not including closing costs. Line B is the loan amount, and Line C is the sales price of the home.

3. **SALES PRICE:**
  A. Cash portion of Sales Price payable by Buyer at closing . . . . $ _____20,000.00_____
  B. Sum of all financing described below (excluding any loan funding
  fee or mortgage insurance premium) . . . . $ _____80,000.00_____
  C. Sales Price (Sum of A and B) . . . . $ _____100,000.00_____

4. Financing

This section indicates how the buyer intends to pay for the property, assuming they are not paying cash. (a) The Third Party Financing box is checked if the buyer intends to get a mortgage in order to pay for the property. The mortgage amount is the sales price minus the buyer's down payment, and does not include any financed loan fees. If the property does not appraise for the sales price, is deemed to be uninsurable, or if the lender requires that certain repairs be made prior to closing, the buyer may terminate the contract. If the contract is contingent upon the buyer's ability to obtain financing, box A is checked, and the Third-Party Financing Addendum is attached. If conventional financing has already been obtained and the buyer wishes to waive the contingency, box B is checked. Note that this box can't be checked for buyers using an FHA or VA loan. (b) Assumption – Assuming a loan is when a buyer takes over the seller's mortgage and begins making their payments. These scenarios are exceedingly rare. (c) Seller Financing – If the seller is acting as a bank and collecting payments from the buyer, section 4C is completed and the Seller Financing Addendum is attached. It is highly recommended that you consult an attorney to produce the legal documents for seller-financed transactions.

---

4. FINANCING (Not for use with reverse mortgage financing): The portion of Sales Price not payable in cash will be paid as follows: (Check applicable boxes below)

☒ A. THIRD PARTY FINANCING: One or more third party mortgage loans in the total amount of $ 80,000.00 (excluding any loan funding fee or mortgage insurance premium).

    (1) Property Approval: If the Property does not satisfy the lenders' underwriting requirements for the loan(s) (including, but not limited to appraisal, insurability and lender required repairs), Buyer may terminate this contract by giving notice to Seller prior to closing and the earnest money will be refunded to Buyer.

    (2) Credit Approval: (Check one box only)

    ☒ (a) This contract is subject to Buyer being approved for the financing described in the attached Third Party Financing Addendum for Credit Approval.

    ☐ (b) This contract is not subject to Buyer being approved for financing and does not involve FHA or VA financing.

☐ B. ASSUMPTION: The assumption of the unpaid principal balance of one or more promissory notes described in the attached TREC Loan Assumption Addendum.

☐ C. SELLER FINANCING: A promissory note from Buyer to Seller of $ _____ , secured by vendor's and deed of trust liens, and containing the terms and conditions described in the attached TREC Seller Financing Addendum. If an owner policy of title insurance is furnished, Buyer shall furnish Seller with a mortgagee policy of title insurance.

---

5. Earnest Money

Earnest money is made payable to the title company. This section specifies the amount of earnest money to be paid, the title company to be used, and any additional earnest money requirements.

---

5. EARNEST MONEY: Upon execution of this contract by all parties, Buyer shall deposit $1,000.00 as earnest money with _____ **Texas Title** _____ , as escrow agent, at _____ **459 Winding Hollow Rd** _____ (address). Buyer shall deposit additional earnest money of $ _____ with escrow agent within _____ days after the effective date of this contract. If Buyer fails to deposit the earnest money as required by this contract, Buyer will be in default.

---

6. Title Policy & Survey

In Texas, it's common for the seller to pay for the buyer's title policy and for the buyer to pay for their lender's title policy. This section indicates who will pay for the policy and the name and address of the title company/issuer. After the title company receives the contract, records are searched by examining the official courthouse records where all recorded documents, judgments, liens, tax assessments, special taxes, and other matters, such as divorce and bankruptcy, are filed. The results of this examination are set forth in a preliminary title report or "commitment" to insure the property. The preliminary title report is delivered to the buyer within 20 days.

The title company requires a survey before a title policy can be issued. Buyers may use the seller's survey if there have been no material changes to the property, like the addition of a pool. The seller submits their survey along with the T-47 Affidavit to the title company within the specified time period. If for some reason the survey is unacceptable, the title company will order a new survey, usually at the buyer's expense. The buyer has time to object to any title or survey defects prior to closing.

As a buyer, you want to state (in section D) ways you may wish to use the property that might not be allowed, like owning a horse. Doing so gives you a way out of the contract if you later learn information that affects your intended use of the property. The section entitled Title Notices discusses the seller's requirement to make certain disclosures to the buyer regarding special tax assessments, whether or not tidewaters affect the property, and whether or not the homeowner is required to belong to a homeowner's association, among others. Buyers have the right to review HOA docs prior to closing, as indicated on the Addendum for Property Subject to Mandatory Membership in an Owner's Association attached to the contract.

6. TITLE POLICY AND SURVEY:

A. TITLE POLICY: Seller shall furnish to Buyer at ☒ Seller's ☐ Buyer's expense an owner policy of title insurance (Title Policy) issued by **Texas Title** _____ (Title Company) in the amount of the Sales Price, dated at or after closing, insuring Buyer against loss under the provisions of the Title Policy, subject to the promulgated exclusions (including existing building and zoning ordinances) and the following exceptions:
   (1) Restrictive covenants common to the platted subdivision in which the Property is located.
   (2) The standard printed exception for standby fees, taxes and assessments.
   (3) Liens created as part of the financing described in Paragraph 4.
   (4) Utility easements created by the dedication deed or plat of the subdivision in which the Property is located.
   (5) Reservations or exceptions otherwise permitted by this contract or as may be approved by Buyer in writing.
   (6) The standard printed exception as to marital rights.
   (7) The standard printed exception as to waters, tidelands, beaches, streams, and related matters.
   (8) The standard printed exception as to discrepancies, conflicts, shortages in area or boundary lines, encroachments or protrusions, or overlapping improvements: ☒ (i) will not be amended or deleted from the title policy; ☐ (ii) will be amended to read, "shortages in area" at the expense of ☒ Buyer ☐ Seller.

B. COMMITMENT: Within 20 days after the Title Company receives a copy of this contract, Seller shall furnish to Buyer a commitment for title insurance (Commitment) and, at Buyer's expense, legible copies of restrictive covenants and documents evidencing exceptions in the Commitment (Exception Documents) other than the standard printed exceptions. Seller authorizes the Title Company to deliver the Commitment and Exception Documents to Buyer at Buyer's address shown in Paragraph 21. If the Commitment and Exception Documents are not delivered to Buyer within the specified time, the time for delivery will be automatically extended up to 15 days or 3 days before the Closing Date, whichever is earlier. If, due to factors beyond Seller's control, the Commitment and Exception Documents are not delivered within the time required, Buyer may terminate this contract and the earnest money will be refunded to Buyer.

C. SURVEY: The survey must be made by a registered professional land surveyor acceptable to the Title Company and Buyer's lender(s). (Check one box only)
   ☐ (1) Within _____5_____ days after the effective date of this contract, Seller shall furnish to Buyer and Title Company Seller's existing survey of the Property and a Residential Real Property Affidavit promulgated by the Texas Department of Insurance (T-47 Affidavit). **If Seller fails to furnish the existing survey or affidavit within the time prescribed, Buyer shall obtain a new survey at Seller's expense no later than 3 days prior to Closing Date.** If the existing survey or affidavit is not acceptable to Title Company or Buyer's lender(s), Buyer shall obtain a new survey at ☐ Seller's ☒ Buyer's expense no later than 3 days prior to Closing Date.
   ☐ (2) Within _____ days after the effective date of this contract, Buyer shall obtain a new survey at Buyer's expense. Buyer is deemed to receive the survey on the date of actual receipt or the date specified in this paragraph, whichever is earlier.
   ☐ (3) Within _____ days after the effective date of this contract, Seller, at Seller's expense shall furnish a new survey to Buyer.

D. OBJECTIONS: Buyer may object in writing to defects, exceptions, or encumbrances to title: disclosed on the survey other than items 6A(1) through (7) above; disclosed in the Commitment other than items 6A(1) through (8) above; or which prohibit the following use or activity: **single family residence** _____ .

Buyer must object the earlier of (i) the Closing Date or (ii) _____ days after Buyer receives the Commitment, Exception Documents, and the survey. Buyer's failure to object within the time allowed will constitute a waiver of Buyer's right to object; except that the requirements in Schedule C of the Commitment are not waived by Buyer. Provided Seller is not obligated to incur any expense, Seller shall cure the timely objections of Buyer or any third party lender within 15 days after Seller receives the objections and the Closing Date will be extended as necessary. If objections are not cured within such 15 day period, this contract will terminate and the earnest money will be refunded to Buyer unless Buyer waives the objections.

E. TITLE NOTICES:

(1) ABSTRACT OR TITLE POLICY: Broker advises Buyer to have an abstract of title covering the Property examined by an attorney of Buyer's selection, or Buyer should be furnished with or obtain a Title Policy. If a Title Policy is furnished, the Commitment should be promptly reviewed by an attorney of Buyer's choice due to the time limitations on Buyer's right to object.

(2) MEMBERSHIP IN PROPERTY OWNERS ASSOCIATION(S): The Property ☒ is ☐ is not subject to mandatory membership in a property owners association(s). If the Property is subject to mandatory membership in a property owners association(s), Seller notifies Buyer under §5.012, Texas Property Code, that, as a purchaser of property in the residential community identified in Paragraph 2A in which the Property is located, you are obligated to be a member of the property owners association(s). Restrictive covenants governing the use and occupancy of the Property and all dedicatory instruments governing the establishment, maintenance, and operation of this residential community have been or will be recorded in the Real Property Records of the county in which the Property is located. Copies of the restrictive covenants and dedicatory instrument may be obtained from the county clerk. **You are obligated to pay assessments to the property owners association(s). The amount of the assessments is subject to change. Your failure to pay the assessments could result in enforcement of the association's lien on and the foreclosure of the Property.**

Section 207.003, Property Code, entitles an owner to receive copies of any document that governs the establishment, maintenance, or operation of a subdivision, including, but not limited to, restrictions, bylaws, rules and regulations, and a resale certificate from a property owners' association. A resale certificate contains information including, but not limited to, statements specifying the amount and frequency of regular assessments and the style and cause number of lawsuits to which the property owners' association is a party, other than lawsuits relating to unpaid ad valorem taxes of an individual member of the association. These documents must be made available to you by the property owners' association or the association's agent on your request.

If Buyer is concerned about these matters, the TREC promulgated Addendum for Property Subject to Mandatory Membership in a Property Owners Association(s) should be used.

(3) STATUTORY TAX DISTRICTS: If the Property is situated in a utility or other statutorily created district providing water, sewer, drainage, or flood control facilities and services, Chapter 49, Texas Water Code, requires Seller to deliver and Buyer to sign the statutory notice relating to the tax rate, bonded indebtedness, or standby fee of the district prior to final execution of this contract.

(4) TIDE WATERS: If the Property abuts the tidally influenced waters of the state, §33.135, Texas Natural Resources Code, requires a notice regarding coastal area property to be included in the contract. An addendum containing the notice promulgated by TREC or required by the parties must be used.

(5) ANNEXATION: If the Property is located outside the limits of a municipality, Seller notifies Buyer under §5.011, Texas Property Code, that the Property may now or later be included in the extraterritorial jurisdiction of a municipality and may now or later be subject to annexation by the municipality. Each municipality maintains a map that depicts its boundaries and extraterritorial jurisdiction. To determine if the Property is located within a municipality's extraterritorial jurisdiction or is likely to be located within a municipality's extraterritorial jurisdiction, contact all municipalities located in the general proximity of the Property for further information.

(6) PROPERTY LOCATED IN A CERTIFICATED SERVICE AREA OF A UTILITY SERVICE PROVIDER: Notice required by §13.257, Water Code: The real property, described in Paragraph 2, that you are about to purchase may be located in a certificated water or sewer service area, which is authorized by law to provide water or sewer service to the properties in the certificated area. If your property is located in a certificated area there may be special costs or charges that you will be required to pay before you can receive water or sewer service. There may be a period required to construct lines or other facilities necessary to provide water or sewer service to your property. You are advised to determine if the property is in a certificated area and contact the utility service provider to determine the cost that you will be required to pay and the period, if any, that is required to provide water or sewer service to your property. The undersigned Buyer hereby acknowledges receipt of the foregoing notice at or before the execution of a binding contract for the purchase of the real property described in Paragraph 2 or at closing of purchase of the real property.

(7) PUBLIC IMPROVEMENT DISTRICTS: If the Property is in a public improvement district, §5.014, Property Code, requires Seller to notify Buyer as follows: As a purchaser of this parcel of real property you are obligated to pay an assessment to a municipality or county for an improvement project undertaken by a public improvement district under Chapter 372, Local Government Code. The assessment may be due annually or in periodic installments. More information concerning the amount of the assessment and the due dates of that assessment may be obtained from the municipality or county levying the assessment. The amount of the assessments is subject to change. Your failure to pay the assessments could result in a lien on and the foreclosure of your property.

(8) TRANSFER FEES: If the Property is subject to a private transfer fee obligation, §5.205, Property Code, requires Seller to notify Buyer as follows: The private transfer fee obligation may be governed by Chapter 5, Subchapter G of the Texas Property Code.

(9) PROPANE GAS SYSTEM SERVICE AREA: If the Property is located in a propane gas system service area owned by a distribution system retailer, Seller must give Buyer written notice as required by §141.010, Texas Utilities Code. An addendum containing the notice approved by TREC or required by the parties should be used.

7. Property Condition

The seller must allow buyers to conduct inspections on the property during reasonable hours. Sellers are required by law to give the buyer a Seller's Disclosure Notice, which describes all known defects to the property. If box B2 is checked, the buyer may cancel the contract within 7 days after receiving this document from the seller. Homes built before 1978 require that a Lead-Based Paint Disclosure be made and attached to the contract.

Section D details specific repairs to be made by seller prior to closing. These are obvious repairs that should be requested prior to an inspection. Checking box number 1 does not waive a buyer's right to inspect the property and negotiate repairs. Section E states that neither party is responsible to make lender required repairs; the contract may be terminated instead. Section F describes the seller's requirement to complete repairs prior to closing. Repairs are to be completed by persons licensed to complete the work. In section H, the buyer may request that the seller pay for a residential home warranty. The buyer selects the company and the coverage and indicates the seller's contribution towards the cost of the policy (usually $400-600 depending on the coverage selected).

7. PROPERTY CONDITION:

A. ACCESS, INSPECTIONS AND UTILITIES: Seller shall permit Buyer and Buyer's agents access to the Property at reasonable times. Buyer may have the Property inspected by inspectors selected by Buyer and licensed by TREC or otherwise permitted by law to make inspections. Seller at Seller's expense shall immediately cause existing utilities to be turned on and shall keep the utilities on during the time this contract is in effect.

B. SELLER'S DISCLOSURE NOTICE PURSUANT TO §5.008, TEXAS PROPERTY CODE (Notice): (Check one box only)

☐ (1) Buyer has received the Notice.

☒ (2) Buyer has not received the Notice. Within ___2___ days after the effective date of this contract, Seller shall deliver the Notice to Buyer. If Buyer does not receive the Notice, Buyer may terminate this contract at any time prior to the closing and the earnest money will be refunded to Buyer. If Seller delivers the Notice, Buyer may terminate this contract for any reason within 7 days after Buyer receives the Notice or prior to the closing, whichever first occurs, and the earnest money will be refunded to Buyer.

☐ (3) The Seller is not required to furnish the notice under the Texas Property Code.

C. SELLER'S DISCLOSURE OF LEAD-BASED PAINT AND LEAD-BASED PAINT HAZARDS is required by Federal law for a residential dwelling constructed prior to 1978.

D. ACCEPTANCE OF PROPERTY CONDITION: "As Is" means the present condition of the Property with any and all defects and without warranty except for the warranties of title and the warranties in this contract. Buyer's agreement to accept the Property As Is under Paragraph 7D(1) or (2) does not preclude Buyer from inspecting the Property under Paragraph 7A, from negotiating repairs or treatments in a subsequent amendment, or from terminating this contract during the Option Period, if any. (Check one box only)

☒ (1) Buyer accepts the Property As Is.

☐ (2) Buyer accepts the Property As Is provided Seller, at Seller's expense, shall complete the the following specific repairs and treatments: _____

_____

(Do not insert general phrases, such as "subject to inspections" that do not identify specific repairs and treatments.)

E. LENDER REQUIRED REPAIRS AND TREATMENTS: Unless otherwise agreed in writing, neither party is obligated to pay for lender required repairs, which includes treatment for wood destroying insects. If the parties do not agree to pay for the lender required repairs or treatments, this contract will terminate and the earnest money will be refunded to Buyer. If the cost of lender required repairs and treatments exceeds 5% of the Sales Price, Buyer may terminate this contract and the earnest money will be refunded to Buyer.

F. COMPLETION OF REPAIRS AND TREATMENTS: Unless otherwise agreed in writing: (i) Seller shall complete all agreed repairs and treatments prior to the Closing Date; and (ii) all required permits must be obtained, and repairs and treatments must be performed by persons who are licensed to provide such repairs or treatments or, if no license is required by law, are commercially engaged in the trade of providing such repairs or treatments. At Buyer's election, any transferable warranties received by Seller with respect to the repairs and treatments will be transfered to Buyer at Buyer's expense. If Seller fails to complete any agreed repairs and treatments prior to the Closing Date, Buyer may exercise remedies under Paragraph 15 or extend the Closing Date up to 5 days if necessary for Seller to complete the repairs and treatments.

G. ENVIRONMENTAL MATTERS: Buyer is advised that the presence of wetlands, toxic substances, including asbestos and wastes or other environmental hazards, or the presence of a threatened or endangered species or its habitat may affect Buyer's intended use of the

Property. If Buyer is concerned about these matters, an addendum promulgated by TREC or required by the parties should be used.

H. RESIDENTIAL SERVICE CONTRACTS: Buyer may purchase a residential service contract from a residential service company licensed by from TREC. If Buyer purchases a residential service contract, Seller shall reimburse Buyer at closing for the cost of the residential service contract in an amount not exceeding $ 400.00 _____. Buyer should review any residential service contract for the scope of coverage, exclusions and limitations. **The purchase of a residential service contract is optional. Similar coverage may be purchased from various companies authorized to do business in Texas.**

8. Broker's Fees

Agreements between the parties and their Realtor representatives are outside this agreement.

8. BROKERS' FEES: All obligations of the parties for payment of brokers' fees are contained in separate written agreements.

9. Closing

The closing date and the obligations of both parties are described in this section. Seller shall clear all encumbrances to the title, and buyer shall bring the required funds to closing.

---

9. CLOSING:

A. The closing of the sale will be on or before _____**January 20**_____, **2015**_____, or within 7 days after objections made under Paragraph 6D have been cured or waived, whichever date is later (Closing Date). If either party fails to close the sale by the Closing Date, the non-defaulting party may exercise the remedies contained in Paragraph 15.

B. At closing:
  (1) Seller shall execute and deliver a general warranty deed conveying title to the Property to Buyer and showing no additional exceptions to those permitted in Paragraph 6 and furnish tax statements or certificates showing no delinquent taxes on the Property.
  (2) Buyer shall pay the Sales Price in good funds acceptable to the escrow agent.
  (3) Seller and Buyer shall execute and deliver any notices, statements, certificates, affidavits, releases, loan documents and other documents reasonably required for the closing of the sale and the issuance of the Title Policy.
  (4) There will be no liens, assessments, or security interests against the Property which will not be satisfied out of the sales proceeds unless securing the payment of any loans assumed by Buyer and assumed loans will not be in default.
  (5) If the Property is subject to a residential lease, Seller shall transfer security deposits (as defined under §92.102, Property Code), if any, to Buyer. In such an event, Buyer shall deliver to the tenant a signed statement acknowledging that the Buyer has received the security deposit and is responsible for the return of the security deposit, and specifying the exact dollar amount of the security deposit.

---

10. Possession

Possession is the date/time that the buyer can actually move into the property. It is common for the seller to have 48 hours to vacate the property after the loan has funded. It is very important that the seller sign a temporary lease agreement if they will occupy the house after funding, even if only for a couple of days. If the seller fails to vacate the property per the terms of the contract, a lease is required to initiate eviction procedures. If the property is vacant, the buyer may take possession immediately after closing/funding.

---

10. POSSESSION:

A. Buyer's Possession: Seller shall deliver to Buyer possession of the Property in its present or required condition, ordinary wear and tear excepted: ☐ upon closing and funding ☒ according to a temporary residential lease form promulgated by TREC or other written lease required by the parties. Any possession by Buyer prior to closing or by Seller after closing which is not authorized by a written lease will establish a tenancy at sufferance relationship between the parties. **Consult your insurance agent prior to change of ownership and possession because insurance coverage may be limited or terminated. The absence of a written lease or appropriate insurance coverage may expose the parties to economic loss.**

B. Leases:
  (1) After the Effective Date, Seller may not execute any lease (including but not limited to mineral leases) or convey any interest in the Property without Buyer's written consent.
  (2) If the Property is subject to any lease to which Seller is a party, Seller shall deliver to Buyer copies of the lease(s) and any move-in condition form signed by the tenant within 7 days after the Effective Date of the contract.

---

11. Special Provisions

Realtors are advised not to write clauses within the Special Provisions of the contract. If your agent is requiring a "respond by" clause in your offer, for example, it will be written in special provisions.

> **11. SPECIAL PROVISIONS:** (Insert only factual statements and business details applicable to the sale. TREC rules prohibit licensees from adding factual statements or business details for which a contract addendum, lease or other form has been promulgated by TREC for mandatory use.)

12. Settlement and Other Expenses

This section details the expenses that are the responsibilities of each party. If the buyer is requesting a seller contribution toward their closing costs, this amount is listed in Section 12A(b).

> **12. SETTLEMENT AND OTHER EXPENSES:**
> A. The following expenses must be paid at or prior to closing:
>   (1) Expenses payable by Seller (Seller's Expenses):
>   (a) Releases of existing liens, including prepayment penalties and recording fees; release of Seller's loan liability; tax statements or certificates; preparation of deed; one-half of escrow fee; and other expenses payable by Seller under this contract.
>   (b) Seller shall also pay an amount not to exceed $ **5,000.00**_____ to be applied in the

> following order: Buyer's Expenses which Buyer is prohibited from paying by FHA, VA, Texas Veterans Land Board or other governmental loan programs, and then to other Buyer's Expenses as allowed by the lender.
>   (2) Expenses payable by Buyer (Buyer's Expenses): Appraisal fees; loan application fees; adjusted origination charges; credit reports; preparation of loan documents; interest on the notes from date of disbursement to one month prior to dates of first monthly payments; recording fees; copies of easements and restrictions; loan title policy with endorsements required by lender; loan-related inspection fees; photos; amortization schedules; one-half of escrow fee; all prepaid items, including required premiums for flood and hazard insurance, reserve deposits for insurance, ad valorem taxes and special governmental assessments; final compliance inspection; courier fee; repair inspection; underwriting fee; wire transfer fee; expenses incident to any loan; Private Mortgage Insurance Premium (PMI), VA Loan Funding Fee, or FHA Mortgage Insurance Premium (MIP) as required by the lender; and other expenses payable by Buyer under this contract.

13. Prorations

Taxes and assessments are prorated through the day of closing. The seller pays for the time they own the house, as does the buyer.

> **13. PRORATIONS:** Taxes for the current year, interest, maintenance fees, assessments, dues and rents will be prorated through the Closing Date. The tax proration may be calculated taking into consideration any change in exemptions that will affect the current year's taxes. If taxes for the current year vary from the amount prorated at closing, the parties shall adjust the prorations when tax statements for the current year are available. If taxes are not paid at or prior to closing, Buyer shall pay taxes for the current year.

14. Casualty Loss

If the property is damaged between the time a contract is executed and closing, the seller is to restore the property to its previous condition. The buyer may terminate the contract if the seller fails to perform as required.

> **14. CASUALTY LOSS:** If any part of the Property is damaged or destroyed by fire or other casualty after the effective date of this contract, Seller shall restore the Property to its previous condition as soon as reasonably possible, but in any event by the Closing Date. If Seller fails to do so due to factors beyond Seller's control, Buyer may (a) terminate this contract and the earnest money will be refunded to Buyer (b) extend the time for performance up to 15 days and the Closing Date will be extended as necessary or (c) accept the Property in its damaged condition with an assignment of insurance proceeds and receive credit from Seller at closing in the amount of the deductible under the insurance policy. Seller's obligations under this paragraph are independent of any other obligations of Seller under this contract.

15. Default

This section describes the seller's rights should the buyer fail to perform as required. Buyers forfeit their earnest money if they fail to comply with the terms of the contract.

> **15. DEFAULT:** If Buyer fails to comply with this contract, Buyer will be in default, and Seller may (a) enforce specific performance, seek such other relief as may be provided by law, or both, or (b) terminate this contract and receive the earnest money as liquidated damages, thereby releasing both parties from this contract. If Seller fails to comply with this contract, Seller will be in default and Buyer may (a) enforce specific performance, seek such other relief as may be provided by law, or both, or (b) terminate this contract and receive the earnest money, thereby releasing both parties from this contract.

16. Mediation

The State of Texas encourages parties to mediate disputes rather than to initiate legal proceedings. The parties are not waiving their right to litigation if a satisfactory outcome is not reached.

> **16. MEDIATION:** It is the policy of the State of Texas to encourage resolution of disputes through alternative dispute resolution procedures such as mediation. Any dispute between Seller and Buyer related to this contract which is not resolved through informal discussion will be submitted to a mutually acceptable mediation service or provider. The parties to the mediation shall bear the mediation costs equally. This paragraph does not preclude a party from seeking equitable relief from a court of competent jurisdiction.

17. Attorney Fees

In the event of a lawsuit, the losing party is to pay all attorney fees.

> **17. ATTORNEY'S FEES:** A Buyer, Seller, Listing Broker, Other Broker, or escrow agent who prevails in any legal proceeding related to this contract is entitled to recover reasonable attorney's fees and all costs of such proceeding.

18. Escrow

In Texas, the title company acts as the neutral third party to the transaction. This section describes in detail the responsibilities and procedures that the title company will follow with regard to expenses, terminating the contract, and notices.

> **18. ESCROW:**
> A. ESCROW: The escrow agent is not (i) a party to this contract and does not have liability for the performance or nonperformance of any party to this contract, (ii) liable for interest on the earnest money and (iii) liable for the loss of any earnest money caused by the failure of any financial institution in which the earnest money has been deposited unless the financial institution is acting as escrow agent.
> B. EXPENSES: At closing, the earnest money must be applied first to any cash down payment, then to Buyer's Expenses and any excess refunded to Buyer. If no closing occurs, escrow agent may: (i) require a written release of liability of the escrow agent from all parties, (ii) require payment of unpaid expenses incurred on behalf of a party, and (iii) only deduct from the earnest money the amount of unpaid expenses incurred on behalf of the party receiving the earnest money.
> C. DEMAND: Upon termination of this contract, either party or the escrow agent may send a release of earnest money to each party and the parties shall execute counterparts of

> the release and deliver same to the escrow agent. If either party fails to execute the release, either party may make a written demand to the escrow agent for the earnest money. If only one party makes written demand for the earnest money, escrow agent shall promptly provide a copy of the demand to the other party. If escrow agent does not receive written objection to the demand from the other party within 15 days, escrow agent may disburse the earnest money to the party making demand reduced by the amount of unpaid expenses incurred on behalf of the party receiving the earnest money and escrow agent may pay the same to the creditors. If escrow agent complies with the provisions of this paragraph, each party hereby releases escrow agent from all adverse claims related to the disbursal of the earnest money.
> D. DAMAGES: Any party who wrongfully fails or refuses to sign a release acceptable to the escrow agent within 7 days of receipt of the request will be liable to the other party for liquidated damages in an amount equal to the sum of: (i) three times the amount of the earnest money; (ii) the earnest money; (iii) reasonable attorney's fees; and (iv) all costs of suit.
> E. NOTICES: Escrow agent's notices will be effective when sent in compliance with Paragraph 21. Notice of objection to the demand will be deemed effective upon receipt by escrow agent.

19. Representations

Seller may be sued for making statements that are untrue. This section also stipulates that the seller may continue to show their home and accept backup offers.

> **19. REPRESENTATIONS:** All covenants, representations and warranties in this contract survive closing. If any representation of Seller in this contract is untrue on the Closing Date, Seller will be in default. Unless expressly prohibited by written agreement, Seller may continue to show the Property and receive, negotiate and accept back up offers.

20. Federal Tax Requirements

If the seller is a foreign person, the buyer may withhold additional funds so that all monies due the IRS can be paid.

> **20. FEDERAL TAX REQUIREMENTS:** If Seller is a "foreign person," as defined by applicable law or if Seller fails to deliver an affidavit to Buyer that Seller is not a "foreign person," then Buyer shall withhold from the sales proceeds an amount sufficient to comply with applicable tax law and deliver the same to the Internal Revenue Service together with appropriate tax forms. Internal Revenue Service regulations require filing written reports if currency in excess of specified amounts is received in the transaction.

21. Notices

Contact information for both the buyer and the seller are listed in this section.

> **21. NOTICES:** All notices from one party to the other must be in writing and are effective when mailed to, hand-delivered at, or transmitted by facsimile or electronic transmission as follows:
>
> **To Buyer at:** 632 Parker Road
> Coppell, TX 75019
> Telephone: (555)123-4567
> Facsimile: _____
>
> E-mail: mrbuyer@me.com
>
> **To Seller at:** 123 Main Street
> Coppell, TX 75019
> Telephone: (555)234-5678
> Facsimile: _____
>
> E-mail: mrseller@me.com

22. Agreement of Parties

The section indicates which amendments are attached to the contract.

23. Termination Period

Buyers are given a period of time (5-14 days) to do their due diligence and may cancel the contract for any reason. The option fee ($50-250) is due within 3 days of contract execution; the seller may terminate the contract if it is not received within this timeframe. If the buyer fails to complete the purchase, the option fee paid to the seller is forfeited. If they complete the purchase, the option fee is refunded at closing. The seller is bound by the terms of the contract and may not terminate the sale.

24. Attorney Notice/Signature Page

The rest of the contract is administrative in nature. There's room to add your attorney's contact information, if you're hiring one. The execution date is the day that all parties have signed the contract. The day after the contract is executed is day one of the option period. What follows is the broker information and receipt page. The listing agent receipts the option money, and the title company receipts the earnest money.

24. CONSULT AN ATTORNEY BEFORE SIGNING: TREC rules prohibit real estate licensees from giving legal advise. READ THIS CONTRACT CAREFULLY.

Buyer's
Attorney is: _____

Seller's
Attorney is: _____

_____

_____

Telephone: _____

Telephone: _____

Facsimile: _____

Facsimile: _____

E-mail: _____

E-mail: _____

EXECUTED the __20th__ **day of** _____January_____ **, 20** __2015__ **(EFFECTIVE DATE).**
(BROKER: FILL IN THE DATE OF FINAL ACCEPTANCE.)

Buyer **Mr. Buyer** _____

Seller **Mr. Seller** _____

Buyer **Mrs. Buyer** _____

Seller **Mrs. Seller** _____

BROKER INFORMATION
(Print name(s) only. Do not sign)

Exclusive Buyer Realty 04488828	Seller Realty 84881283
Other Broker Firm License No.	Listing Broker Firm License No.

represents	[X] Buyer only as Buyer's agent	represents	[ ] Seller and Buyer as an intermediary
	[ ] Seller as Listing Broker's subagent		[X] Seller only as Seller's agent

Your EBA's Boss (123) 456-7890	Seller Agent's Boss (123) 432-9877
Name of Associate's Licensed Supervisor Telephone	Name of Associate's Licensed Supervisor Telephone

Betty Buyer Agent (123) 567-8777	Sally Seller Agent (123) 848-0249
Associate's Name Telephone	Listing Associate's Name Telephone

EBA Address	Seller Agent Address
Other Broker's Address (123) 838-2883 Facsimile	Listing Broker's Office Address Facsimile

Coppell TX 75019	Dallas TX 750939
City State Zip	City State Zip

sarahsedgwick@me.com	sallyselleragent@me.com
Associate's Email Address	Listing Associate's Email Address

	Selling Associate's Name Telephone
	Name of Selling Associate's Licensed Supervisor Telephone
	Selling Associate's Office Address Facsimile
	City State Zip
	Selling Associate's Email Address

Listing Broker has agreed to pay Other Broker ____3.000%____ of the total sales price when the Listing Broker's fee is received. Escrow agent is authorized and directed to pay other Broker from Listing Broker's fee at closing.

OPTION FEE RECEIPT

Receipt of $ _____ (Option Fee) in the form of _____ is acknowledged.

_____
Seller or Listing Broker   Date

CONTRACT AND EARNEST MONEY RECEIPT

Receipt of [ ] Contract and [ ] $_____ Earnest Money in the form of _____
is acknowledged.
Escrow Agent: _____   Date: _____

By: _____
_____   Email Address
_____   Telephone: _____
Address
_____   Facsimile: _____
City   State   Zip

Third Party Financing Addendum

The Third Party Financing Addendum For Credit Approval is a simple, two-page document that allows the buyer to terminate the earnest money contract if financing cannot be obtained within a specific time frame, usually

15-20 days. It also discloses to the seller the type of financing being used (Conventional, Texas Veterans, FHA, VA, or USDA) and puts a cap on the interest rate and fees associated with the loan.

2-10-2014

THIRD PARTY FINANCING ADDENDUM FOR CREDIT APPROVAL
(Not for use with Reverse Mortgage Financing)

TO CONTRACT CONCERNING THE PROPERTY AT

123 Main Street   Coppell

(Street Address and City)

Buyer shall apply promptly for all financing described below and make every reasonable effort to obtain credit approval for the financing (Credit Approval). Buyer shall furnish all information and documents required by lender for Credit Approval. Credit Approval will be deemed to have been obtained when (1) the terms of the loan(s) described below are available and (2) lender determines that Buyer has satisfied all of lender's requirements related to Buyer's assets, income and credit history. If Buyer cannot obtain Credit Approval, Buyer may give written notice to Seller within _____ days after the effective date of this contract and this contract will terminate and the earnest money will be refunded to Buyer. **If Buyer does not give such notice within the time required, this contract will no longer be subject to Credit Approval. Time is of the essence for this paragraph and strict compliance with the time for performance is required.**

NOTE: Credit Approval does not include approval of lender's underwriting requirements for the Property, as specified in Paragraph 4.A.(1) of the contract.

Each note must be secured by vendor's and deed of trust liens.

CHECK APPLICABLE BOXES:

☒ A. CONVENTIONAL FINANCING:
  ☒ (1) A first mortgage loan in the principal amount of $ 180,000.00 _____ (excluding any financed PMI premium), due in full in _____30_____ year(s), with interest not to exceed ___4.500___ % per annum for the first __30__ year(s) of the loan with Adjusted Origination Charges as shown on Buyer's Good Faith Estimate for the loan not to exceed _____1.000_____ % of the loan.
  □ (2) A second mortgage loan in the principal amount of $ _____ (excluding any financed PMI premium), due in full in _____ year(s), with interest not to exceed _____ % per annum for the first _____ year(s) of the loan with Adjusted Origination Charges as shown on Buyer's Good Faith Estimate for the loan not to exceed _____ % of the loan.

□ B. TEXAS VETERANS LOAN: A loan(s) from the Texas Veterans Land Board of $ _____ for a period in the total amount of _____ years at the interest rate established by the Texas Veterans Land Board.

□ C. FHA INSURED FINANCING: A Section _____ FHA insured loan of not less than $ _____ (excluding any financed MIP), amortizable monthly for not less than _____ years, with interest not to exceed _____ % per annum for the first _____ year(s) of the loan with Adjusted Origination Charges as shown on Buyer's Good Faith Estimate for the loan not to exceed _____ % of the loan. As required by HUD-FHA, if FHA valuation is unknown, *"It is expressly agreed that, notwithstanding any other provision of this contract, the purchaser (Buyer) shall not be obligated to complete the purchase of the Property described herein or to incur any penalty by forfeiture of earnest money deposits or otherwise unless the purchaser (Buyer) has been given in accordance with HUD/FHA or VA requirements a written statement issued by the Federal Housing Commissioner, Department of Veterans Affairs, or a Direct Endorsement Lender setting forth the appraised value of the Property of not less than $ _____ . The purchaser (Buyer) shall have the privilege and option of proceeding with consummation of the contract without regard to the amount of the*

Initialed for identification by Buyer_____ _____ and Seller_____ _____ TREC NO. 40-6

Third Party Financing Condition Addendum Concerning   Page 2 of 2 2-10-2014

123 Main Street, Coppell,   75019
(Address of Property)

appraised valuation. The appraised valuation is arrived at to determine the maximum mortgage the Department of Housing and Urban Development will insure. HUD does not warrant the value or the condition of the Property. The purchaser (Buyer) should satisfy himself/herself that the price and the condition of the Property are acceptable."

❑ D. VA GUARANTEED FINANCING: A VA guaranteed loan of not less than $ _____ (excluding any financed Funding Fee), amortizable monthly for not less than _____ years, with interest not to exceed _____ % per annum for the first _____ year(s) of the loan with Adjusted Origination Charges as shown on Buyer's Good Faith Estimate for the loan not to exceed _____ % of the loan.

VA NOTICE TO BUYER: "It is expressly agreed that, notwithstanding any other provisions of this contract, the Buyer shall not incur any penalty by forfeiture of earnest money or otherwise or be obligated to complete the purchase of the Property described herein, if the contract purchase price or cost exceeds the reasonable value of the Property established by the Department of Veterans Affairs. The Buyer shall, however, have the privilege and option of proceeding with the consummation of this contract without regard to the amount of the reasonable value established by the Department of Veterans Affairs."

If Buyer elects to complete the purchase at an amount in excess of the reasonable value established by VA, Buyer shall pay such excess amount in cash from a source which Buyer agrees to disclose to the VA and which Buyer represents will not be from borrowed funds except as approved by VA. If VA reasonable value of the Property is less than the Sales Price, Seller may reduce the Sales Price to an amount equal to the VA reasonable value and the sale will be closed at the lower Sales Price with proportionate adjustments to the down payment and the loan amount.

❑ E. USDA GUARANTEED FINANCING: A USDA-guaranteed loan of not less than $ _____ (excluding any financed Funding Fee), amortizable monthly for not less than _____ years, with interest not to exceed _____ % per annum for the first _____ year(s) of the loan with Adjusted Origination Charges as shown on Buyer's Good Faith Estimate for the loan not to exceed _____ % of the loan.

Buyer hereby authorizes any lender to furnish to the Seller or Buyer or their representatives information relating only to the status of Credit Approval of Buyer.

Buyer Mr. Buyer _____   Seller Mr. Seller _____

Buyer Mrs. Buyer _____   Seller Mrs. Seller _____

This form has been approved by the Texas Real Estate Commission for use with similarly approved or promulgated contract forms. Such approval relates to this form only. TREC forms are intended for use only by trained real estate licensees. No representation is made as to the legal validity or adequacy of any provision in any specific transactions. It is not intended for complex transactions. Texas Real Estate Commission, P.O. Box 12188, Austin, TX 78711-2188, (512) 936-3000 (http://www.trec.texas.gov) TREC No. 40-6. This form replaces TREC No. 40-5.

TREC NO. 40-6

Produced with zipForm® by zipLogix 18070 Fifteen Mile Road, Fraser, Michigan 48026 www.zipLogix.com   Book

Seller's Temporary Lease Agreement

It is customary to allow the seller 48 hours to vacate the property after closing. Always have the seller sign the Seller's Temporary Residential

Lease agreement to stipulate how long they can stay and to specify the penalty for not being out on time. If for some reason they refuse to move, a lease is required to evict them from the property.

PROMULGATED BY THE TEXAS REAL ESTATE COMMISSION (TREC)   12-05-2011
(NOTICE: For use only when SELLER occupies the property for no more than 90 days AFTER the closing)

SELLER'S TEMPORARY RESIDENTIAL LEASE

1. **PARTIES:** The parties to this Lease are _____ Mr. Buyer, Mrs. Buyer _____

   (Landlord) and _____ Mr. Seller, Mrs. Seller _____ (Tenant).

2. **LEASE:** Landlord leases to Tenant the Property described in the Contract between Landlord as Buyer and Tenant as Seller known as 123 Main Street, Coppell,   75019 _____ (address).

3. **TERM:** The term of this Lease commences on the date the sale covered by the Contract is closed and funded and terminates February 6, 2015 8pm , unless terminated earlier by reason of other provisions.

4. **RENTAL:** Tenant shall pay to Landlord as rental $ _____ per day (excluding the day of closing and funding) with the full amount of rental for the term of the Lease to be paid at the time of funding of the sale. Tenant will not be entitled to a refund of rental if this Lease terminates early due to Tenant's default or voluntary surrender of the Property.

5. **DEPOSIT:** Tenant shall pay to Landlord at the time of funding of the sale $ _____ as a deposit to secure performance of this Lease by Tenant. Landlord may use the deposit to satisfy Tenant's obligations under this Lease. Landlord shall refund any unused portion of the deposit to Tenant with an itemized list of all deductions from the deposit within 30 days after Tenant (a) surrenders possession of the Property and (b) provides Landlord written notice of Tenant's forwarding address.

6. **UTILITIES:** Tenant shall pay all utility charges except _____ n/a _____ which Landlord shall pay.

7. **USE OF PROPERTY:** Tenant may use the Property only for residential purposes. Tenant may not assign this Lease or sublet any part of the Property.

8. **PETS:** Tenant may not keep pets on the Property except _____ existing _____ .

9. **CONDITION OF PROPERTY:** Tenant accepts the Property in its present condition and state of repair at the commencement of the Lease. Upon termination, Tenant shall surrender the Property to Landlord in the condition required under the Contract, except normal wear and tear and any casualty loss.

10. **ALTERATIONS:** Tenant may not alter the Property or install improvements or fixtures without the prior written consent of the Landlord. Any improvements or fixtures placed on the Property during the Lease become the Property of Landlord.

11. **SPECIAL PROVISIONS:** Tenant to leave home in clean, move-in condition.

12. **INSPECTIONS:** Landlord may enter at reasonable times to inspect the Property. Tenant shall provide Landlord door keys and access codes to allow access to the Property during the term of Lease.

13. **LAWS:** Tenant shall comply with all applicable laws, restrictions, ordinances, rules and regulations with respect to the Property.

14. **REPAIRS AND MAINTENANCE:** Except as otherwise provided in this Lease, Tenant shall bear all expense of repairing and maintaining the Property, including but not limited to the yard, trees and shrubs, unless otherwise required by the Texas Property Code. Tenant shall promptly repair at Tenant's expense any damage to the Property caused directly or indirectly by any act or omission of the Tenant or any person other than the Landlord, Landlord's agents or invitees.

Initialed for identification by Landlord _____ and Tenant _____   TREC NO. 15-5

Seller's Temporary Residential Lease

123 Main Street
Coppell,   75019
(Address of Property)

Page 2 of 2 12-05-2011

15. INDEMNITY: Tenant indemnifies Landlord from the claims of all third parties for injury or damage to the person or property of such third party arising from the use or occupancy of the Property by Tenant. This indemnification includes attorney's fees, costs and expenses incurred by Landlord.

16. INSURANCE: Landlord and Tenant shall each maintain such insurance on the contents and Property as each party may deem appropriate during the term of this Lease. NOTE: CONSULT YOUR INSURANCE AGENT; POSSESSION OF THE PROPERTY BY SELLER AS TENANT MAY CHANGE INSURANCE POLICY COVERAGE.

17. DEFAULT: If Tenant fails to perform or observe any provision of this Lease and fails, within 24 hours after notice by Landlord, to commence and diligently pursue to remedy such failure, Tenant will be in default.

18. TERMINATION: This Lease terminates upon expiration of the term specified in Paragraph 3 or upon Tenant's default under this Lease.

19. HOLDING OVER: Tenant shall surrender possession of the Property upon termination of this Lease. Any possession by Tenant after termination creates a tenancy at sufferance and will not operate to renew or extend this Lease. Tenant shall pay $ 100.00 per day during the period of any possession after termination as damages, in addition to any other remedies to which Landlord is entitled.

20. ATTORNEY'S FEES: The prevailing party in any legal proceeding brought under or with respect to this Lease is entitled to recover from the non-prevailing party all costs of such proceeding and reasonable attorney's fees.

21. SMOKE ALARMS: The Texas Property Code requires Landlord to install smoke alarms in certain locations within the Property at Landlord's expense. Tenant expressly waives Landlord's duty to inspect and repair smoke alarms.

22. SECURITY DEVICES: The requirements of the Texas Property Code relating to security devices do not apply to a residential lease for a term of 90 days or less.

23. CONSULT YOUR ATTORNEY: Real estate licensees cannot give legal advice. This Lease is intended to be legally binding. READ IT CAREFULLY. If you do not understand the effect of this Lease, consult your attorney BEFORE signing.

24. NOTICES: All notices from one party to the other must be in writing and are effective when mailed to, hand-delivered at, or transmitted by facsimile or electronic transmission as follows:

To Landlord: Buyer's info here   **To Tenant:** Seller's info here

Telephone: _____   Telephone: _____
Facsimile: _____   Facsimile: _____
E-mail: _____   E-mail: _____

Landlord Mr. Buyer   Tenant Mr. Seller

Landlord Mrs. Buyer   Tenant Mrs. Seller

TREC NO. 15-5

Book

Home Owners Association Addendum

The Addendum for Property Subject to Mandatory Membership in a Property Owners Association allows the buyer to request or waive their right to receive a copy of the bylaws and rules of the association prior to closing. The fees associated with obtaining these documents are negotiable, but are generally a seller's expense.

PROMULGATED BY THE TEXAS REAL ESTATE COMMISSION (TREC) 08-18-2014

ADDENDUM FOR PROPERTY SUBJECT TO MANDATORY MEMBERSHIP IN A PROPERTY OWNERS ASSOCIATION
(NOT FOR USE WITH CONDOMINIUMS)
ADDENDUM TO CONTRACT CONCERNING THE PROPERTY AT

123 Main Street   Coppell
(Street Address and City)

Lakes of Coppell
(Name of Property Owners Association, (Association) and Phone Number)

A. SUBDIVISION INFORMATION: "Subdivision Information" means: (i) a current copy of the restrictions applying to the subdivision and bylaws and rules of the Association, and (ii) a resale certificate, all of which are described by Section 207.003 of the Texas Property Code.

(Check only one box):

☒ 1. Within ___15___ days after the effective date of the contract, Seller shall obtain, pay for, and deliver the Subdivision Information to the Buyer. If Seller delivers the Subdivision Information, Buyer may terminate the contract within 3 days after Buyer receives the Subdivision Information or prior to closing, whichever occurs first, and the earnest money will be refunded to Buyer. If Buyer does not receive the Subdivision Information, Buyer, as Buyer's sole remedy, may terminate the contract at any time prior to closing and the earnest money will be refunded to Buyer.

☐ 2. Within _____ days after the effective date of the contract, Buyer shall obtain, pay for, and deliver a copy of the Subdivision Information to the Seller. If Buyer obtains the Subdivision Information within the time required, Buyer may terminate the contract within 3 days after Buyer receives the Subdivision Information or prior to closing, whichever occurs first, and the earnest money will be refunded to Buyer. If Buyer, due to factors beyond Buyer's control, is not able to obtain the Subdivision Information within the time required, Buyer may, as Buyer's sole remedy, terminate the contract within 3 days after the time required or prior to closing, whichever occurs first, and the earnest money will be refunded to Buyer.

☐ 3. Buyer has received and approved the Subdivision Information before signing the contract. Buyer ☐ does ☐ does not require an updated resale certificate. If Buyer requires an updated resale certificate, Seller, at Buyer's expense, shall deliver it to Buyer within 10 days after receiving payment for the updated resale certificate from Buyer. Buyer may terminate this contract and the earnest money will be refunded to Buyer if Seller fails to deliver the updated resale certificate within the time required.

☐ 4. Buyer does not require delivery of the Subdivision Information.

The title company or its agent is authorized to act on behalf of the parties to obtain the Subdivision Information ONLY upon receipt of the required fee for the Subdivision Information from the party obligated to pay.

B. MATERIAL CHANGES. If Seller becomes aware of any material changes in the Subdivision Information, Seller shall promptly give notice to Buyer. Buyer may terminate the contract prior to closing by giving written notice to Seller if: (i) any of the Subdivision Information provided was not true; or (ii) any material adverse change in the Subdivision Information occurs prior to closing, and the earnest money will be refunded to Buyer.

C. FEES: Except as provided by Paragraphs A, D and E, Buyer shall pay any and all Association fees or other charges associated with the transfer of the Property not to exceed $ _150.00_ and Seller shall pay any excess.

D. DEPOSITS FOR RESERVES: Buyer shall pay any deposits for reserves required at closing by the Association.

E. AUTHORIZATION: Seller authorizes the Association to release and provide the Subdivision Information and any updated resale certificate if requested by the Buyer, the Title Company, or any broker to this sale. If Buyer does not require the Subdivision Information or an updated resale certificate, and the Title Company requires information from the Association (such as the status of dues, special assessments, violations of covenants and restrictions, and a waiver of any right of first refusal), ☐ Buyer ☒ Seller shall pay the Title Company the cost of obtaining the information prior to the Title Company ordering the information.

NOTICE TO BUYER REGARDING REPAIRS BY THE ASSOCIATION: The Association may have the sole responsibility to make certain repairs to the Property. If you are concerned about the condition of any part of the Property which the Association is required to repair, you should not sign the contract unless you are satisfied that the Association will make the desired repairs.

Buyer _Mr. Buyer_ _____   Seller _Mr. Seller_ _____

Buyer _Mrs. Buyer_ _____   Seller _Mrs. Seller_ _____

The form of this addendum has been approved by the Texas Real Estate Commission for use only with similarly approved or promulgated forms of contracts. Such approval relates to this contract form only. TREC forms are intended for use only by trained real estate licensees. No representation is made as to the legal validity or adequacy of any provision in any specific transactions. It is not intended for complex transactions. Texas Real Estate Commission, P.O. Box 12188, Austin, TX 78711-2188, (512) 936-3000 (www.trec.texas.gov) TREC No. 36-8. This form replaces TREC No. 36-7.

TREC NO. 36-8

HelpUBuy America, 106 N. Denton Tap Road Coppell, TX 75019   Phone: 214.734.3863   Fax: 866-593-9533   Book
Alysse Musgrave   Produced with zipForm® by zipLogix 18070 Fifteen Mile Road, Fraser, Michigan 48026 www.zipLogix.com

{ 6 }

Inspections & Property Condition

You definitely need to hire a professional inspector to go through every square inch of the house and report the findings. Your inspector should be experienced and come recommended from a friend, co-worker, or your Realtor.

> *Be aware, however, of potential conflicts of interest if you rely on a recommendation from your Realtor. Hopefully, your Realtor will give you a list of inspectors to choose from, and you can make your own choice.*

I recommend inspectors based on the quality of their reports, but I don't have personal relationships with them, nor have I even met most of them. I don't attend inspections in order to give my clients the opportunity to discuss the condition of the house with a neutral party to the transaction. The inspector gets paid whether the deal closes or not! If I have a question about an item on the report, I email the inspector and always include my client in the communication. The inspectors work for my clients, not for me, and I welcome their advice and expertise.

A good inspection should take about three to four hours, depending on the size of the house. In the end you will have a list of items that are in need of repair or replacement, and you will have learned how to maintain the property. Your inspector should go through each item with you. Be certain you understand the report so that you can make good choices when requesting repairs from the seller.

Which Repairs to Request

Even when you are buying new construction, you don't get a perfect house. Don't expect the seller to agree to all the repairs. Once you submit your repair request, negotiations are on again. When negotiating repairs, consider the following:

Roof

Find out the condition of the roof and try to estimate the remaining life. If there is existing damage from hail, for example, be sure that the seller files a claim with their insurance company, and do not close until the roof is either replaced or the money is held in escrow (the title company holds the money and pays the roofer once the repair has been made). This is non-negotiable since you may have a problem getting homeowner's insurance on the property if there is existing damage.

> *Do not incur any additional expenses until this issue is resolved! If you need to walk away from the house, you want to lose as little money as possible.*

Sprinkler

With the exception of broken sprinkler heads, I don't like my clients to assume the risk of a broken sprinkler system. Repairs can be expensive and leaks hard to locate. Have the seller make any repairs before closing.

Appliances

Only built-in appliances are included in the sale of a home. Ovens, ranges, built-in microwaves, and dishwashers are relatively low cost items to repair/replace. If these items are working when you close on the house, they will be covered by any home warranty that you have in place.

Foundation

With very few exceptions, I advise my clients to walk away from homes that have existing or previous foundation repairs.

> *One of the riskiest things you can do is to buy a home that needs, or has had, a foundation repair.*

Not only can the house be damaged during the repair (particularly the plumbing), but also you can't be certain that the repair will hold. In addition, when it's time to sell, you must – by law – disclose the repair to potential buyers of the home. Many potential buyers won't want to assume the risk, and you'll have no choice but to sell the property below market value. While it's true that some foundation repair companies offer lifetime transferrable warranties on their work, you can't trust the foundation repair company to honor your claim or to be in business as long as you own the house. *Leave foundation issues to the investors and the buyers who have some bad karma coming their way.*

Air Conditioners and Heaters

Both air conditioning and heating units can be extremely costly to repair or replace, and you should insist that the seller make any necessary repairs before closing. It is especially important to clean the a/c coils if they are found to be dirty. Coils become dirty when the homeowner fails to change the filters on a regular basis. Because this is considered to be a maintenance item, cleaning the coils is typically excluded from your home warranty and is an expense that you shouldn't have to incur.

Windows

One of the most common issues I see pertains to double-pane windows. When air gets between the two panes of glass in a double-pane window, it can lead to condensation and fog. The only fix is to replace the glass. I typically advise my clients to request the repair of foggy windows when they are in highly visible locations. If the majority of the windows are faulty, I recommend replacement of all the windows or cash in lieu of replacement, since the cost to replace all of the windows will be several thousand dollars.

Cosmetics

Paint, faucets, flooring, and sealant/trim are what I consider to be cosmetic items. I always recommend that my clients take care of these items themselves after the sale. The seller usually tries to save money by making the repairs themselves and the results are not always good. If the home is in need of substantial cosmetic updating, you need to pay less for the house or get a decorating allowance.

Plumbing

With the exception of small leaks or minor items, the seller needs to make all plumbing repairs and assume the risk. This includes repairs to the hot water heater, especially if the water heater is in the attic.

Repair Allowances

Under certain circumstances, you may wish to ask for cash in lieu of repairs or to ask for cash in addition to certain repairs. As previously mentioned, there are certain repairs that are best handled by the buyer after closing. Many times sellers would prefer not to have to deal with the inconvenience of repairing the property; psychologically they have already moved on to the next house. Talk to your agent about how much it might cost to repair certain items and then see what the sellers are willing to do.

When to Walk Away

If you have done your homework in advance, and if you are working with a skilled career agent, the inspection should not reveal any big surprises. However, if something major does come up during inspection, you have some decisions to make. It's reasonable to expect to buy a home with a solid roof and working electrical, plumbing, and cooling/heating systems. If any of these items need to be replaced, you should be buying the home below market value (that is, the low end of the range on your CMA) or requesting that the seller make the repair or provide a repair allowance. These problems can be fixed. The question is, who pays for it? If the issue is something major, it is time to cut your losses and move on; you certainly don't want to buy someone else's problem.

So what is considered "major?" You should walk away from anything that would prevent a future buyer from wanting to buy the house. If a future buyer wouldn't want it, you shouldn't want it either. Things like foundation problems, toxic mold, multiple termite treatments, violent deaths on the property, a basement that floods frequently, asbestos, and radon are all good reasons to pass on buying the property.

Air conditioners and roofs can be replaced. The stench of a double homicide in the house lives forever.

{ 7 }

All About Mortgages

I started talking about predatory lending and improper homebuying practices over 20 years ago. I received a lot of hate mail and even anonymous threats from mortgage 'professionals' (aka mob bosses) who did not want their secrets revealed.

Today, lenders are required to be far more transparent in their pricing and loan programs. While it's still very possible to rip off an uneducated, unprepared borrower, mortgage law makes it much harder to rip off someone who knows how the system works.

I spend a lot of time educating my buyers before we ever really talk seriously about buying. The following pages are intended to "give it to you in a nutshell." Education is vital if we are going to eliminate predatory lending practices. Let's get started.

Some Definitions

Mortgage brokers hire loan officers to sell loans to consumers. They have accounts with wholesale lenders, who are the actual source of the funds. Each day, the wholesale lenders will provide the mortgage brokers, and all their loan officers, with wholesale rate sheets. The mortgage broker decides how much profit he or she wants to make on each loan and creates a retail rate sheet. The loan officers sell from the retail rate sheet. The difference between the wholesale rate, the retail rate, and the closing fees makes up the lender's profit margin.

Mortgage Brokers vs. Banks

When shopping for a loan, you can use a mortgage broker or deal directly with the bank. What follows is a simplification of the differences between the two.

Mortgage Brokers

A mortgage broker is extremely knowledgeable in the field of mortgages. They know the market and keep track of which lender might be offering a discount or have a unique product. When you work with a broker, they compare wholesale mortgage rates for you from all kinds of banks and lending institutions; they can often get you a better price than if you went to the bank directly. It's not uncommon for a broker to sell you a Wells Fargo loan, for example, at a lower price than you could get if you went directly to Wells Fargo! Because there is less bureaucracy with a mortgage broker, the process is generally more streamlined and efficient (assuming an equal level of competency). Mortgage brokers are *required* to disclose to you their commission (called a Yield Spread Premium), so you will always know the profit they are making on your loan.

A good mortgage broker is worth his or her weight in gold. A bad one, well...

Banks

Bank of America, Wells Fargo, and Chase are examples of big banks that can loan you money to buy a house. These banks have the capital to permanently keep your mortgage in their portfolio. You get a mortgage through Chase and you make your payments to Chase until the loan is paid off.

Smaller, regional banks don't have the long-term funds available to keep your loans for very long. They issue mortgages that conform to industry standards and sell them to investors almost immediately, locking in their profits.

Banks differ from brokers in that they don't have to disclose their profits (Yield Spread Premium) to the borrower. It's the goal of many brokers to meet the qualifications necessary to call themselves a bank so they can avoid this disclosure requirement. YSPs are a controversial topic in the industry.

Big banks are known for being inefficient and expensive. In my area, many listing agents advise their seller/clients *not* to accept a buyer's contract when their lender comes from one of these institutions, and I agree with their reasoning. While a small bank or a broker can close a transaction in 3 or 4 weeks, the big banks often take 6 weeks or longer, and they still often miss the closing date. Their loan officers tend to be untrained order takers who are not really qualified to offer financial advice to buyers. The loan files move – slowly and inaccurately – from department to department. Dealing with big banks adds an unnecessary layer of stress to the transaction.

Loan officers that work for brokers or small banks are far more knowledgeable and service-oriented; I have someone to call if there's a problem that needs to be resolved. The same isn't true with a big bank.

Do yourself a favor. Stick with a small, regional bank or a broker. You'll be glad you did.

How Lenders Make Money

Mortgage brokers make money several different ways. They can manipulate these potential profit avenues all day long to come up with their desired profit. The following sections describe the various ways mortgage brokers make money.

Closing costs

This includes fees for applications, credit reports, appraisals, processing, underwriting, document preparation, and so forth. These fees are sometimes referred to as "junk fees."

Origination fees

Origination fees are usually one percent of the loan amount. This is simply a fee that the broker charges for writing the loan.

Discount Points

Points are prepaid interest. They are usually only charged when the buyer wants an interest rate that is below market rates. Discount points are expressed as a percentage of the loan amount. One point is equal to one percent of the loan amount, three points is equal to three percent of the loan amount, and so forth. Example: If you are quoted an interest rate of 7.25 percent with zero points, but you have your heart set on an interest rate of seven percent, you could pay one point and buy the interest rate down to this amount.

Yield Spread Premiums (YSP)

YSPs are rebates paid by wholesale lenders to mortgage brokers for writing loans that are above "par" or market interest rates. If the par rate is eight percent, but your mortgage broker can get you to pay 8.5 percent, the wholesale lender will pay your broker an extra commission called a Yield Spread Premium. YSPs can help consumers who are short on cash. They can pay a higher interest rate and have their mortgage broker pay some of their closing costs. There is nothing inherently wrong with YSPs, unless they are used for improper purposes.

How You Can Get Ripped Off

Closing costs

Some closing costs are legitimate fees for services performed by a third party. Your credit report and appraisal are examples of legitimate fees - some of these fees are collected upfront. Some legitimate fees (like processing fees) are collected at closing. Are all other fees junk fees? It is impossible to say. There are an endless number of ways that lenders can manipulate closing costs. They can waive most of your closing costs and charge you a higher interest rate. You still pay, of course; you simply do not pay up front. They can charge you for services that are never performed. They can charge you $400 for an appraisal that costs $250.

Origination Fee

There are legitimate costs associated with loan origination, and your lender is entitled to make a fair profit. To charge a one percent origination is fine, but to charge a one percent origination fee in conjunction with inflated or fabricated closing costs and premium interest rates could be considered excessive.

Discount points

Discount points are points paid for their stated purpose. Reducing the consumer's interest rate is a good purpose, but a dishonest lender can quote you a certain rate at the time of the loan application and produce something quite different at the closing table. For example, you may be told that because of a past credit problem you do not qualify for the best rate. You are "forced" to either buy down the interest rate by paying additional discount points, or you agree to a higher rate, in which case the broker receives a rebate in the form of a Yield Spread Premium, which is discussed next.

Yield Spread Premiums

If your loan officer can get you to pay a higher-than-market interest rate, they get a "rebate" called a Yield Spread Premium. This is how it happens. You agree to a 30-year loan at 6.5 percent. Since interest rates change daily, your loan officer will not lock in your interest rate right away. They will "float" your loan until there is a little dip in rates, and then they will lock in your loan - let's say at 6.25 percent.

Since your loan officer has you committed to pay 6.5 percent, he or she will get an extra commission for selling you a loan at a higher-than-market interest rate. These commissions are often in the multiple thousands! An upfront and ethical loan officer would have rebated you the YSP or given you the 6.25 percent interest rate.

Since the lender (brokers only) is not required to disclose this extra profit to you until closing, you are none the wiser until it is too late to do anything about it. YSPs provide a useful option to some borrowers. For those with little cash, YSPs make no-cost mortgages possible because the lender pays closing costs. For those who expect to be in their house only a few years, YSPs permit a favorable exchange of higher rate for lower fees. However, in the hands of unscrupulous lenders, they can cost the borrower thousands and thousands of dollars.

How Can All This Happen?

Mortgage brokers are regulated by RESPA and other state agencies, and the good news is that highly positive changes have been made in the past few years. Lenders can no longer charge more than 3% in fees, and disclosures made to the borrower are more meaningful and easier to understand. Most closing costs can no longer increase by more than 10%; the lender is required to rebate any excess overages back to the borrower at closing. They can't pull a "bait and switch" by offering you one interest rate upfront and raising it at the closing table (now they can do it 3 days before closing, as you'll read later). But it can still be tough to enforce the rules, so fraud still exists. Anxious, emotional homebuyers are very easy to manipulate. The best thing you can do as a potential buyer is to educate yourself and hire a great agent to help you.

The Lender's Dilemma

Interest rates are based on risk; the better your credentials, the lower your interest rate. Because it is a risk-based system, you will not learn your final interest rate until after you make a formal loan application and until you lock your rate. It's a "chicken or the egg" scenario. Lenders don't want to commit to pricing until you make a formal loan application, and buyers don't want to commit to a loan without knowing the costs.

Closing costs are disclosed to borrowers on a document called a Loan Estimate (LE).

There was a time when a lender could provide a potential borrower a Good Faith Estimate (now known as a Loan Estimate) and it was understood that the figures were just estimates. But beginning in 2010, the lender is bound by most of the fees that they quote. As such, many lenders now provide an "Initial Fees Worksheet" or a "Financing Scenario" while you shop for a mortgage instead of the Loan Estimate which commits them to the prices that they quote.

> *By giving you a Financing Scenario, rather than a Loan Estimate, the lender is giving you a price without actually making a commitment.*

So what does this all mean? It means that the Department of Housing and Urban Development's (HUD) recent initiatives to make shopping for a loan easier for buyers have failed, and borrowers are still going to have to take extra steps to avoid being ripped off.

> *A lender is not necessarily a crook simply because they give you an Initial Fees Worksheet instead of an LE; this is the policy of some of the most honest and competent lenders I know. It's a matter of practicality and risk reduction.*

However, it is a manipulation of the system, and the system doesn't make it easy for borrowers to tell the difference between the good guys and the bad guys. Follow the procedures discussed later to ensure you won't be ripped off.

Qualified Mortgages & Ability to Repay

Lenders are now encouraged to ensure that borrowers have the ability to repay their mortgages. In return, lenders will be protected from borrower lawsuits so long as they issue "safe" mortgages that follow guidelines. Certain loans are not allowed, including the following:

- Interest-only loans
- Negative amortization
- Large balloon payments
- Loans that are longer than 30 years
- Excessive upfront points & fees
- A debt to income ration of more than 43%

As the Consumer Financial Protection Bureau (CFPB) website puts it: "The ability-to-repay rule is intended to prevent consumers from getting trapped in mortgages that they cannot afford and to prevent lenders from making loans that consumers do not have the ability to repay. It's that simple." Enough said.

How to Find a Lender

Chances are you will hear that the best place to find a lender is through a friend or family member. I disagree. Your friends and family probably have no idea if they were ripped off, and unless they work in the industry they are no match for a predatory lender. Some say that your agent is *not* a good resource; again, I disagree. Your agent knows which lenders can close on time, which lenders deliver what they promise, and which lenders treat customers fairly. The lenders that agents recommend go out of their way to treat buyers well so those agents will continue to send them clients. Ask your agent for a list of their favorite lenders and then give them all a call, but remember that you are never required to use any vendor that your Realtor recommends.

Shopping for a Loan

After you have found a house, contact several lenders and ask for a quote. The loan officer will either refer you to their online loan application site or take information from you over the phone, and then send you a Loan Estimate or an Initial Fees Worksheet. Compare the documents, with your agent's help if needed, and pursue the least expensive ones *that can close on time.*

Remember, if the pricing isn't given to you on a Loan Estimate, it can change. More on that ahead.

THIS STEP IS IMPORTANT

Send your top choices the following information. Do so in writing (email is fine) with a return receipt:

- Your full name(s)
- Your monthly income(s)
- Your Social Security number(s)
- The property address
- The loan amount
- The property value or sales price

Providing them with *all* this information triggers the requirement that a Loan Estimate be delivered within three days.

The lender is required by RESPA (mortgage law) to give you a Loan Estimate and all the price guarantees that come along with it.

Changes in income, sales price, loan program, or locking your rate can trigger a new Loan Estimate, rendering the original one obsolete. The final Loan Estimate is the one that must match your settlement statement at closing.

After comparing several Loan Estimates, select the best loan for you and notify the loan originator that you would like to proceed with the loan. Keep your original Loan Estimate so you can compare it with the final settlement costs stated on your Closing Disclosure, although these documents include a comparison of what was quoted and what was delivered. Some charges cannot be raised, and your lender must reimburse you if those charges were illegally or erroneously increased. Others can go up by a ten percent margin, and the lender has to reimburse you for any excess.

> *The loan officer may want you to give him a credit card number or a check so that he can order the appraisal. Do NOT give them a dime until you are 100 percent certain that you plan to use them. YOU ARE NOT REQUIRED TO USE A LENDER SIMPLY BECAUSE THEY SEND YOU A LOAN ESTIMATE.*

Getting the Best Deal

The Annual Percentage Rate (APR) is supposed to make comparing and selecting the best mortgage rates easier, and mortgage lenders are required by law to disclose it. It's calculated by taking the loan amount, adding in the cost of financing (interest and closing costs), and converting it to a percentage. Online lenders love to advertise their low APRs, and they count on the borrower not understanding that shopping for a loan by selecting the lowest APR is a flawed plan.

The problem with shopping for a loan this way is that certain fees may or may not be included in the APR calculation, depending upon the lender, and it's hard to make an apples-to-apples comparison. The APR can help you compare loans with different rates and fees in order to select the best one, but it is an imperfect tool.

> *A better method is for you to calculate your own APR. Use an online APR calculator to do the math.*

Calculating your own APR based on the Loan Estimates given to you by a few lenders allows you to control the data used in the calculation.

Here's another smart way to shop for a loan. Follow the steps above to determine the interest rate for which you are most likely to qualify. For the sake of discussion, assume you are quoted an interest rate of 4% on a 30-year fixed mortgage with zero points and $2,000 in closing costs. Contact other lenders and ask to see the costs associated with a 4%, 30-year fixed mortgage with zero points. Then compare the closing costs.

Rate Shopping & Your Credit Score

Looking for a mortgage will cause multiple lenders to request your credit report, even though you are looking for only one loan. The credit scoring system ignores mortgage loan inquires made in the 30 days prior to scoring. Thus, if you find a loan within 30 days, the rate shopping will not affect your score.

Points vs. Rate

When choosing a mortgage, you generally have the option to pay points (prepaid interest) in exchange for a lower interest rate. If you plan to stay in the home for more than five to seven years, it is usually in your favor to pay the points. In the long run, the lower interest rate will save you more money. Ask your loan officer to run an analysis for you to help you decide.

Loan Estimate Form

The Consumer Financial Protection Bureau (CFPB) requires easy-to-understand mortgage disclosure forms that clearly lay out the terms of a mortgage for a homebuyer. The new "Know Before You Owe" mortgage forms known as the Loan Estimate (LE) and Closing Disclosure (CE) re-placed the Good Faith Estimate (GFE) and HUD-1 in October 2015. These new forms help consumers understand their options, choose the deal that's best for them, and avoid costly surprises at the closing table.

The new Loan Estimate document is so well written that it needs no explanation. Really. The Loan Estimate is three pages long. The first page contains information identifying the borrower and loan, the loan terms, the projected monthly payments, the total estimated closing costs, and the total estimated cash needed to close. The second page breaks down the closing costs in more detail and includes information on prepaid and escrowed amounts, as well as detail on the cash needed to close. The third page includes a summary of loan costs over five years (to provide for a comparison with other loan products), along with required disclosures regarding the delivery of a copy of an appraisal to the borrower, whether the loan is assumable, whether homeowner's insurance is required, late payment fee information, and whether the loan servicing may be transferred. The third page also contains a signature block for consumers to confirm receipt of the disclosure.

FICUS BANK
4321 Random Boulevard · Somecity, ST 12340

Save this Loan Estimate to compare with your Closing Disclosure.

Loan Estimate

		LOAN TERM	30 years
		PURPOSE	Purchase
DATE ISSUED	2/15/2013	PRODUCT	Fixed Rate
APPLICANTS	Michael Jones and Mary Stone	LOAN TYPE	⊠ Conventional ☐ FHA ☐ VA ☐_____
	123 Anywhere Street	LOAN ID #	123456789
	Anytown, ST 12345	RATE LOCK	☐ NO ⊠ YES, until 4/16/2013 at 5:00 p.m. EDT
PROPERTY	456 Somewhere Avenue		*Before closing, your interest rate, points, and lender credits can*
	Anytown, ST 12345		*change unless you lock the interest rate. All other estimated*
SALE PRICE	$180,000		*closing costs expire on 3/4/2013 at 5:00 p.m. EDT*

Loan Terms		Can this amount increase after closing?
Loan Amount	$162,000	**NO**
Interest Rate	3.875%	**NO**
Monthly Principal & Interest *See Projected Payments below for your Estimated Total Monthly Payment*	$761.78	**NO**
		Does the loan have these features?
Prepayment Penalty		**YES** · As high as **$3,240** if you pay off the loan during the first 2 years
Balloon Payment		**NO**

Loan Estimate - Top of Page One

Projected Payments

Payment Calculation	Years 1-7	Years 8-30
Principal & Interest	$761.78	$761.78
Mortgage Insurance	+ 82	+ —
Estimated Escrow Amount can increase over time	+ 206	+ 206
Estimated Total Monthly Payment	**$1,050**	**$968**

		This estimate includes	In escrow?
Estimated Taxes, Insurance & Assessments Amount can increase over time	**$206** a month	[X] Property Taxes [X] Homeowner's Insurance [ ] Other: See Section G on page 2 for escrowed property costs. You must pay for other property costs separately.	YES YES

Costs at Closing

Estimated Closing Costs	$8,054	Includes $5,672 in Loan Costs + $2,382 in Other Costs – $0 in Lender Credits. See page 2 for details.
Estimated Cash to Close	$16,054	Includes Closing Costs. See Calculating Cash to Close on page 2 for details.

Visit **www.consumerfinance.gov/mortgage-estimate** for general information and tools.

LOAN ESTIMATE   PAGE 1 OF 3 • LOAN ID # 123456789

Loan Estimate - Bottom of Page One

Closing Cost Details

Loan Costs

A. Origination Charges	$1,802
.25 % of Loan Amount (Points)	$405
Application Fee	$300
Underwriting Fee	$1,097

B. Services You Cannot Shop For	$672
Appraisal Fee	$405
Credit Report Fee	$30
Flood Determination Fee	$20
Flood Monitoring Fee	$32
Tax Monitoring Fee	$75
Tax Status Research Fee	$110

Other Costs

E. Taxes and Other Government Fees	$85
Recording Fees and Other Taxes	$85
Transfer Taxes	

F. Prepaids	$867
Homeowner's Insurance Premium (6 months)	$605
Mortgage Insurance Premium (months)	
Prepaid Interest ($17.44 per day for 15 days @ 3.875%)	$262
Property Taxes (months)	

G. Initial Escrow Payment at Closing	$413
Homeowner's Insurance $100.83 per month for 2 mo.	$202
Mortgage Insurance per month for mo.	
Property Taxes $105.30 per month for 2 mo.	$211

H. Other	$1,017
Title – Owner's Title Policy (optional)	$1,017

I. TOTAL OTHER COSTS (E + F + G + H)	$2,382

Loan Estimate - Top of Page Two

C. Services You Can Shop For	$3,198
Pest Inspection Fee	$135
Survey Fee	$65
Title – Insurance Binder	$700
Title – Lender's Title Policy	$535
Title – Settlement Agent Fee	$502
Title – Title Search	$1,261

D. TOTAL LOAN COSTS (A + B + C)	$5,672

J. TOTAL CLOSING COSTS	$8,054
D + I	$8,054
Lender Credits	

Calculating Cash to Close

Total Closing Costs (J)	$8,054
Closing Costs Financed (Paid from your Loan Amount)	$0
Down Payment/Funds from Borrower	$18,000
Deposit	– $10,000
Funds for Borrower	$0
Seller Credits	$0
Adjustments and Other Credits	$0
Estimated Cash to Close	$16,054

Loan Estimate - Bottom of Page Two

Additional Information About This Loan

LENDER	Ficus Bank		MORTGAGE BROKER	
NMLS/__ LICENSE ID			NMLS/__ LICENSE ID	
LOAN OFFICER	Joe Smith		LOAN OFFICER	
NMLS/__ LICENSE ID	12345		NMLS/__ LICENSE ID	
EMAIL	joesmith@ficusbank.com		EMAIL	
PHONE	123-456-7890		PHONE	

Comparisons   Use these measures to compare this loan with other loans.

In 5 Years	$56,582	Total you will have paid in principal, interest, mortgage insurance, and loan costs.
	$15,773	Principal you will have paid off.
Annual Percentage Rate (APR)	4.274%	Your costs over the loan term expressed as a rate. This is not your interest rate.
Total Interest Percentage (TIP)	69.45%	The total amount of interest that you will pay over the loan term as a percentage of your loan amount.

Loan Estimate - Top of Page Three

Other Considerations

Appraisal	We may order an appraisal to determine the property's value and charge you for this appraisal. We will promptly give you a copy of any appraisal, even if your loan does not close. You can pay for an additional appraisal for your own use at your own cost.
Assumption	If you sell or transfer this property to another person, we ☐ will allow, under certain conditions, this person to assume this loan on the original terms. ☒ will not allow assumption of this loan on the original terms.
Homeowner's Insurance	This loan requires homeowner's insurance on the property, which you may obtain from a company of your choice that we find acceptable.
Late Payment	If your payment is more than *15* days late, we will charge a late fee of *5% of the monthly principal and interest payment.*
Refinance	Refinancing this loan will depend on your future financial situation, the property value, and market conditions. You may not be able to refinance this loan.
Servicing	We intend ☐ to service your loan. If so, you will make your payments to us. ☒ to transfer servicing of your loan.

Confirm Receipt

By signing, you are only confirming that you have received this form. You do not have to accept this loan because you have signed or received this form.

Applicant Signature	Date	Co-Applicant Signature	Date

Loan Estimate - Bottom of Page Three

Types of Loans

Over the past few years, subprime and no money down financing programs have disappeared, and the mortgage industry has gone back to traditional mortgage programs. FHA and Conventional financing are the most traditional type of financing.

If you can qualify for conventional financing, it is the least expensive option. If not, pursue an FHA. Some people mistakenly believe that FHA loans are strictly for low-income borrowers. This is absolutely not true. People of all incomes obtain FHA loans.

The following sections highlight the requirements and benefits of each type of loan.

Conventional vs. FHA Financing

FHA Financing

FHA is a government insured mortgage program, meaning the government guarantees the loan if the borrower defaults. This type of financing was part of the government's initiative to encourage homeownership. The credit requirements are much more relaxed, and you can often get a loan with a 580 credit score. The minimum down payment on an FHA loan is 3.5 percent of the purchase price, and they *do* accept gifted funds from a close relative.

The FHA program is becoming more and more popular lately, since it is easier to qualify for than a conventional mortgage. FHA is, however, more expensive than conventional financing.

Mortgage Insurance Premium (MIP)

Mortgage insurance is an insurance policy that protects lenders in the event a borrower defaults on the loan. FHA loans require two different types of mortgage insurance premiums for most buyers. The first is called the Up-front Mortgage Insurance Premium (UFMIP), and is a percentage (approximately 1.5 percent) of the total amount that you are borrowing. It can be paid in cash at closing or can be rolled into the loan amount. The second type of mortgage insurance is called monthly MIP (Mortgage Insurance Premium). MIP premiums are paid as part of your monthly mortgage payments. In years past, MIP could be cancelled once the borrower had roughly 20% equity in the home, either through appreciation or principal reduction. *Those days are gone.* In 2013 the rules changed. FHA borrowers who put less than 10% down will have to pay the MIP premium for the life of the loan. I'll repeat this statement for emphasis.

FHA borrowers who put down less than 10% will have to pay the annual MIP for the life of the loan.

If you have a credit score of 680 or higher, but little money in the bank, a better loan for you is the Conventional 97, discussed later.

Conventional Financing

A conventional loan is a loan that is not insured by the government; the lender takes on the risk of losing money in the event that the borrower defaults on the mortgage. Conventional mortgages are for those borrowers with better credit; credit scores need to be in the 680 plus range. Expect to put down between 3 percent and 20 percent when you purchase a home using a conventional mortgage.

Private Mortgage Insurance (PMI)

Most lenders require private mortgage insurance (PMI) when the buyer puts down less than 20% of the home's value upon purchase. It allows borrowers to make smaller down payments, making it possible for them to buy a home sooner since they don't have to save up as much money. Unlike MIP that is associated with an FHA loan, there is no upfront premium to pay with a conventional loan. In addition, PMI can be cancelled when the homeowner has sufficient equity in the property (usually 20-22 percent), either through appreciation or principal reduction.

Conventional 97

The Conventional 97 program requires a minimum 3 percent down payment, based on the lower of the home's appraised value or purchase price. On a $150,000 house, this translates to a down payment of $4,500 (3%), compared to $5,250 on an FHA (3.5%). In addition to the other benefits of a conventional loan mentioned above, (no upfront premium and the ability to cancel PMI with 20% equity), down payment funds can often be gifted from third parties.

If you have a high enough credit score (680+), this is a far better loan than the FHA.

Fixed Rate vs. Adjustable Rate

Fixed rate or adjustable rate refers to the interest rate, which can either remain the same throughout the life of the loan or change periodically. Fixed and adjustable rates are discussed below.

Fixed Rate

A fixed-rate mortgage has an interest rate that never changes. This means, unlike an adjustable-rate mortgage, you are protected from higher monthly mortgage payments if interest rates suddenly rise. If mortgage rates drop, however, you do not benefit from the lower rate unless you refinance.

Even though the interest rate is fixed, the amount that you will pay depends on the mortgage term. The most common terms are 30, 20, and 15 years. The 30-year mortgage is the most popular because it has the lowest monthly payment. The tradeoff is that the loan overall costs a lot more because you are paying extra interest for ten or fifteen years. Additionally, the interest rate of a 30-year mortgage is typically higher than with a shorter term.

If you're interested in a shorter-term loan but are concerned about the higher payment, go with the 30-year mortgage and follow the advice in the section titled "Prepaying Your Mortgage" later in the book.

Adjustable-Rate Mortgages

ARMs are attractive to some because the initial rate is low, which allows the borrower to qualify for a larger loan. They are risky because your mortgage interest rate (and therefore your mortgage payment) changes frequently over the life of the loan. Some are structured so that interest rates can more than double in just a few years. If you don't plan to live in a property long enough for the rates to rise, than an ARM might be a good choice. Otherwise, especially given today's low interest rates, stick with a fixed-rate mortgage.

USDA/Rural Housing Loans

USDA loans are insured by the Department of Agriculture. Their most notable feature is their option for "no money down" or "100% financing." The purpose of the loan is to spur development of rural areas, and both the property and the buyer must qualify for USDA financing. Beyond that, they are very similar to other types of loans.

With the exception of VA financing, USDA loans are really the only source of no money down financing these days. Why? Because when a homeowner doesn't have any skin in the game (home equity), there is a much higher chance that they will walk away from their mortgage and go into foreclosure. Most lenders are no longer comfortable with that level of risk. In addition, no money down means the buyer is rolling their closing costs into the loan; it will take them years to build up any equity. If they can no longer afford their payments, and they don't have enough equity in the property to cover their selling expenses, they are stuck. They have no choice but to walk away from their mortgage.

Buying a home in a USDA neighborhood is a risk, even if you don't obtain a USDA loan. A large number of foreclosures brings down the value of the entire neighborhood. The neighborhood might be beautiful when you move in, but as time goes on and your neighbors begin to neglect and ultimately lose their homes, it will change. Your charming neighborhood and the value of your home will be diminished when 50% of your neighbors abandon their homes.

There is a reason that buyers must be enticed (or bribed) to move out to rural areas. These neighborhoods are far from everything, which means resale can be difficult. The pool of potential buyers in a rural area is much smaller than in neighborhoods that are closer to modern conveniences. Proceed with caution if you plan to buy a home this way.

Your Loan Step-by-Step

The following is a description of what happens, step-by-step, after you choose a lender and complete your loan application:

1. **Documentation is Ordered** - Within twenty-four hours of application, your lender will order a credit report, appraisal, verifications of employment and funds to close, and any other supporting documentation that is necessary.

2. **Wait for Documentation** - After you submit your supporting documentation, the loan officer checks for any potential problems and requests additional items as needed. It can take two to three weeks for all the items to be received.

3. **Loan Submission** - Once all the necessary documentation is in, the loan officer reviews the current programs to ensure you get the best rate and terms possible. The loan processor then puts the loan package together and submits it to the underwriter for approval.

4. **Loan Approval** - Loan approval generally takes anywhere from 24 to 72 hours. All parties are notified of the approval and any loan conditions that must be received before the loan can close. The loan approval is the beginning of the closing process.

5. **Documents are Created** - Within one to three days after the loan approval, the loan documents (including the note and deed of trust) are completed and sent to the title company. The escrow officer calls the borrowers to come in when the papers are ready for final signature. At this time, the borrowers are told how much money they will need to bring in to close the loan.

6. **Funding** - Once all parties have signed the loan documents, they are returned to the lender, who reviews the package. If all the forms have been properly executed, the check is issued to fund the loan.

7. **Recording** - When the title company receives the funding check from the lender, they make the lender's security for the loan a matter of public record. They do this by recording the note and deed of trust at the county recorder's office. Escrow is now officially closed and the house is yours!

{ 8 }

A Moment of Silence

After repairs have been agreed upon and you have made a formal loan application with your lender, things can get very quiet. Some buyers mistakenly believe that nothing is happening, when in fact there are many, many things taking place behind the scenes. All the items below must be completed and approved before closing:

Title Insurance

Title insurance is protection against loss arising from problems connected with the title to your property. Before you purchased your home, several people may have owned the property, and even more may have owned the land. This is called the "chain of title." When the property sold, if someone forged a signature (perhaps a former spouse), or if there were unpaid taxes or other liens, there is a cloud on the title. A cloud on the title indicates that there is a lien or claim that needs to be cleared before it can be sold.

Title insurance covers the insured party for any claims and legal fees that arise from such issues. If you buy a house, for example, and someone's former spouse claims that he or she never signed the paperwork to sell the house, you are covered by title insurance. The lender-required insurance pro-tects the lender up to the amount of the mortgage, but it doesn't protect your equity in the property. For that you need an owner's title policy for the full value of the home. In many areas, sellers pay for owner policies as part of their obligation to deliver good title to the buyer. In other areas, borrowers must buy it as an add-on to the lender policy.

Appraisal

An appraiser, an objective third party to the transaction, performs the ap-praisal. The appraiser's job is to give their professional opinion of the market value of a home. Lenders use the appraisal to determine the appropriate loan amount. A lender will not lend more than the value of the home, and the ap-praised value is used to determine common loan ratios that factor into the loan approval process, such as loan to value, or LTV. You are entitled to a copy of the appraisal; after all, you paid $350-400 for it. If your lender does not send you a copy on their own, ask them for it. They are required to give it to you.

Survey

A property survey is a sketch or map of a property showing its boundaries and other physical features (see below). They also show the relative location of a house, shed, and/or other building(s) and fences on the property, and it usually includes the position of any public or municipal easements. Mortgage lenders generally require a property survey before they will loan money for a mortgage, and many title insurers require this as well. In Texas, the seller may share their survey with the buyer if there have been no material changes to the property. This saves the buyer several hundred dollars at closing.

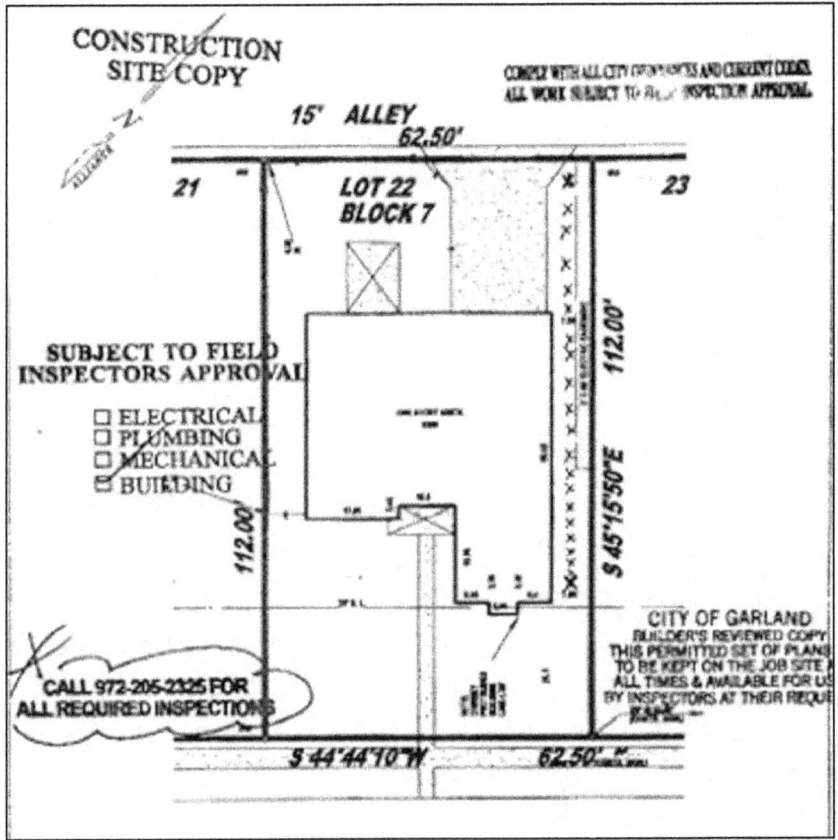

Loan Approval

The steps of the loan process were discussed earlier. To recap, after you turn in all your supporting documents, your loan is turned over to the underwriter for final approval. After all the underwriter's conditions are met, your file is declared "clear to close." The documents are then prepared and sent to the title company.

Homeowner's Association (HOA)

If you are buying in a neighborhood with an HOA, the association will be notified, and the paperwork will be transferred to your name. If the seller has any outstanding fees or fines, they will be collected prior to closing. After closing, you'll receive an invoice directly from the HOA when the next year's fees are due.

Homeowner's Insurance

It is your responsibility to obtain homeowner's insurance before closing. Homeowner's insurance protects a homeowner against loss from fire and other hazards that may impair the value of their home. It is a lot easier to shop for homeowner's insurance than a mortgage because premiums change only occasionally, so the price you are quoted is very likely the price you will pay.

In shopping for the lowest premium, you need to be very careful to compare apples to apples.

Compare two items: the deductible and the coverage.

The "deductible" is the loss that is the homeowner's responsibility. Only losses above that amount are insured. Higher deductibles carry lower premiums. But lenders limit the amount of deductible they will allow – one percent is a typical maximum.

The "coverage" dictates the maximum loss the policy will pay. There are four levels of coverage:

- actual cash value (lowest coverage)
- replacement cost
- extended replacement cost
- guaranteed replacement cost (highest coverage, but not always available).

Higher coverage carries higher premiums. Lenders typically require coverage of 125 percent of the cost of replacement, though this may be scaled down if the land accounts for an unusually large part of the house value.

Call several insurance agents for quotes, and when you have made your selection, have the insurance agent send a "binder" to the title company. The title company is responsible for collecting money from you and paying for the policy at closing.

Home Warranty

A home warranty is a contract between a home warranty company and a homeowner that provides discounted repair or replacement on a variety of items in a home. You can choose your level of coverage to include the basic items like the furnace, air conditioning, plumbing, and electrical systems, or you can add coverage for appliances, pools, refrigerators, and others.

If something in your house that was working at closing breaks, you call the home warranty company. The home warranty sends over the right service provider for the job. The repair is made or the component is replaced, and the homeowner only pays the cost of the service call, usually $60-100.

There are many different home warranty companies and many different levels of service. There are varied exclusions in their contracts, so review them carefully when you make your selection, and match the right coverage to the house you are buying. For example, if the water heater works but is a little dated, be sure that the policy you pick will replace it.

I always negotiate a home warranty for my buyer/clients (except for new homes), and so should you unless the home you are buying is in pristine condition and everything is new.

{ 9 }

Walk-Throughs & Lease Backs

A typical closing takes an average of 30 days. It's not uncommon for a homeowner to stop cleaning and maintaining the home between the period of time that they accept an offer and moving day. The seller may also need a few days, or even longer, after closing to vacate the property. The following section discusses these scenarios.

Pre-Closing Walk-Through

A walk-through is a final inspection of the home before closing, and I recommend two of them. The first should be done forty-eight hours before closing to verify that all the agreed upon repairs have been completed (get receipts!) and to make sure that there hasn't been any damage to the property since you were last there.

> *You do not want to wait until an hour before closing to express dissatisfaction with the condition of the home since the seller needs time to make corrections.*

Take your camera and take pictures of anything wrong with the property, and let your agent share them with the seller's side.

The second walk-through should be done immediately before closing just to be sure everything is okay before you sign your papers. This is something I generally do for my buyers since they are busy at the bank and often are coming right from work.

If something major is wrong with the house, don't close.

"Major" means something big, like the air conditioner doesn't work, the house was vandalized, there was a hailstorm that damaged the roof, and other similar conditions. The house needs to be turned over to you in the same condition as you last saw it, and the repairs must have been completed. Otherwise, don't close.

If you have small grievances, your agent can negotiate money for you to make the repair after closing, or the title company can hold back some of the seller's proceeds in escrow until the situation has been resolved. It is during times like this that you need a good agent to represent your interests.

Temporary Lease Backs

Quite often, the seller does not move out of the property until after closing and funding; it's risky for them to leave until they are 100 percent certain the deal will close. For the period of time after funding when the buyer officially owns the house, to the time that the seller moves out, the seller is living in the buyer's house.

You absolutely must have the sellers sign a temporary lease agreement, which means they are your tenants until they move out.

With a proper lease, the seller can be evicted if they refuse to move out. Make certain the lease specifies that the house needs to be left in clean, move-in condition. The word "clean" is subjective, of course. I generally suggest that buyers plan on hiring a cleaning service and carpet cleaners before they move in and to consider it a closing cost. You might get lucky and the seller will leave you a spotless house, but don't count on it.

{ 10 }

Closing

The closing is when all the paperwork is signed and all funds are disbursed. A title company or settlement company facilitates the entire process. The title company is also the issuer of your title insurance policy. As a mostly neutral third party to the transaction, the settlement company has many responsibilities including:

- Cashing the buyer's earnest money check and holding the money in a trust account
- Managing the paperwork between the buyer's agent and the seller's agent, the lender, insurance companies, and home warranty providers.
- Coordinating the funding of the loan
- Paying off the seller's loan
- Preparing the Closing Disclosure
- Disbursing the seller's checks and the agent's commissions
- Prorating annual property taxes and other obligations

Once your loan is fully approved and you are clear to close, your lender will send papers and instructions to the title/settlement company. Based on those instructions, the closer will prepare your closing statement and distribute it to all the parties involved for approval. You can compare your Loan Estimate to the actual closing statement to see how close your lender's estimate was to actual figures. If there are any big surprises, discuss them with your agent and lender immediately. Also be certain that you received a credit for any deposits you put down for earnest money, any option fees, prepaid appraisals, and so forth. Again, your agent should be extremely familiar with this document and can help you. You will need to bring a cashier's check in the appropriate amount to closing, along with a picture ID; be sure to keep your funds readily accessible in a local account.

Once approved, both buyer and seller will sign the documents, and the funds will be distributed to the appropriate parties. When everyone has been paid, you get the keys to your new house!

The Closing Disclosure

Consumers will receive this form three business days before closing on a loan. This form provides a detailed accounting of the transaction. Providing the borrower this important information well ahead of closing enables them to have time to understand their loan costs in an unpressured environment rather than at the closing table. It also eliminates frantic last minute trips to the bank to get a cashier's check an hour before closing and gives the parties time to troubleshoot mistakes.

If there are changes to the Closing Disclosure between the time it is issued and closing, *depending on the nature of the change*, the creditor must provide an updated Closing Disclosure with another three-business-day waiting period. The changes that require the creditor to provide an updated Closing Disclosure and an additional three-business-day waiting period are: (1) changes to the APR greater than 1/8 of a percent, (2) changes to the loan product, or (3) the addition of a prepayment penalty. Less significant changes can be disclosed on an updated Closing Disclosure without the need for an additional three-business-day waiting period.

> *Fraud alert! A predatory lender might promise one thing on the Loan Estimate and later lock the borrower into a loan that is more expensive. They can claim that the borrower didn't qualify for the loan terms that were originally promised, and they can do so as long as they re-disclose the terms of the loan to the borrower and allow for a three-day waiting period before closing. In the hands of a predatory lender, it's a bait and switch. A three-day waiting period isn't that long! Few buyers will cancel their transaction based on a ¼ point increase on their loan, but that ¼ point translates into thousands of dollars for the lender. This is where the reputation of the lender really matters!*

The Closing Disclosure is five pages long. The first page is similar to the first page of the Loan Estimate and contains information that identifies the borrower and loan, loan terms, monthly payments, and the total closing costs and total cash needed to close.

The second page contains a list of closing costs, including whether the borrower, seller, or another party pays each particular cost. The third page includes a calculation of the cash needed to close and a summary of the borrower's transaction and seller's transaction.

Pages four and five contain additional loan disclosures and contact information for the creditor, brokers, and settlement agent. The additional disclosures address whether the loan is assumable, negative amortization information, late payment fees, escrow requirements, and a lot more. The fifth page also includes a calculation of the total payments, finance charges, amount financed, and total interest percentage over the term of the loan. Finally, the fifth page also contains a signature block for consumers to confirm receipt of the disclosure.

Like the Loan Estimate form, the Closing Disclosure is incredibly easy to understand. A sample of this form is depicted below.

Closing Disclosure

This form is a statement of final loan terms and closing costs. Compare this document with your Loan Estimate.

Closing Information

Date Issued	4/15/2013
Closing Date	4/15/2013
Disbursement Date	4/15/2013
Settlement Agent	Epsilon Title Co.
File #	12-3456
Property	456 Somewhere Ave
	Anytown, ST 12345
Sale Price	$180,000

Transaction Information

Borrower	Michael Jones and Mary Stone
	123 Anywhere Street
	Anytown, ST 12345
Seller	Steve Cole and Amy Doe
	321 Somewhere Drive
	Anytown, ST 12345
Lender	Ficus Bank

Loan Information

Loan Term	30 years
Purpose	Purchase
Product	Fixed Rate
Loan Type	☒ Conventional ☐ FHA
	☐ VA ☐ _____
Loan ID #	123456789
MIC #	000654321

Loan Terms		Can this amount increase after closing?
Loan Amount	$162,000	NO
Interest Rate	3.875%	NO
Monthly Principal & Interest See Projected Payments below for your Estimated Total Monthly Payment	$761.78	NO
		Does the loan have these features?
Prepayment Penalty		YES • **As high as $3,240** if you pay off the loan during the first 2 years
Balloon Payment		NO

Closing Disclosure - Top of Page 1

Projected Payments

Payment Calculation		Years 1-7		Years 8-30
Principal & Interest		$761.78		$761.78
Mortgage Insurance	+	82.35	+	—
Estimated Escrow Amount can increase over time	+	206.13	+	206.13
Estimated Total Monthly Payment		**$1,050.26**		**$967.91**

		This estimate includes	In escrow?
Estimated Taxes, Insurance & Assessments Amount can increase over time See page 4 for details	**$356.13** a month	[X] Property Taxes [X] Homeowner's Insurance [X] Other: Homeowner's Association Dues See Escrow Account on page 4 for details. You must pay for other property costs separately.	YES YES NO

Costs at Closing

Closing Costs	$9,712.10	Includes $4,694.05 in Loan Costs + $5,018.05 in Other Costs – $0 in Lender Credits. See page 2 for details.
Cash to Close	**$14,147.26**	Includes Closing Costs. See Calculating Cash to Close on page 3 for details.

Closing Disclosure- Bottom of Page 1

Calculating Cash to Close

Use this table to see what has changed from your Loan Estimate.

	Loan Estimate	Final	Did this change?	
Total Closing Costs (J)	$8,054.00	$9,712.10	YES	· See Total Loan Costs (D) and Total Other Costs (I)
Closing Costs Paid Before Closing	$0	– $29.80	YES	· You paid these Closing Costs before closing
Closing Costs Financed (Paid from your Loan Amount)	$0	$0	NO	
Down Payment/Funds from Borrower	$18,000.00	$18,000.00	NO	
Deposit	– $10,000.00	– $10,000.00	NO	
Funds for Borrower	$0	$0	NO	
Seller Credits	$0	– $2,500.00	YES	· See Seller Credits in Section L
Adjustments and Other Credits	$0	– $1,035.04	YES	· See details in Sections K and L
Cash to Close	$16,054.00	$14,147.26		

Closing Disclosure - Top of Page 2

Summaries of Transactions   Use this table to see a summary of your transaction.

BORROWER'S TRANSACTION		SELLER'S TRANSACTION	
K. Due from Borrower at Closing	**$189,762.30**	**M. Due to Seller at Closing**	**$180,080.00**
01 Sale Price of Property	$180,000.00	01 Sale Price of Property	$180,000.00
02 Sale Price of Any Personal Property Included in Sale		02 Sale Price of Any Personal Property Included in Sale	
03 Closing Costs Paid at Closing (J)	$9,682.30	03	
04		04	
Adjustments		05	
05		06	
06		07	
07		08	
Adjustments for Items Paid by Seller in Advance		**Adjustments for Items Paid by Seller in Advance**	
08 City/Town Taxes to		09 City/Town Taxes to	
09 County Taxes to		10 County Taxes to	
10 Assessments to		11 Assessments to	
11 HOA Dues 4/15/13 to 4/30/13	$80.00	12 HOA Dues 4/15/13 to 4/30/13	$80.00
12		13	
13		14	
14		15	
15		16	
L. Paid Already by or on Behalf of Borrower at Closing	**$175,615.04**	**N. Due from Seller at Closing**	**$115,665.04**
01 Deposit	$10,000.00	01 Excess Deposit	
02 Loan Amount	$162,000.00	02 Closing Costs Paid at Closing (J)	$12,800.00
03 Existing Loan(s) Assumed or Taken Subject to		03 Existing Loan(s) Assumed or Taken Subject to	
04		04 Payoff of First Mortgage Loan	$100,000.00
05 Seller Credit	$2,500.00	05 Payoff of Second Mortgage Loan	
Other Credits		06	
06 Rebate from Epsilon Title Co.	$750.00	07	
07		08 Seller Credit	$2,500.00
Adjustments		09	
08		10	
09		11	
10		12	
11		13	
Adjustments for Items Unpaid by Seller		**Adjustments for Items Unpaid by Seller**	
12 City/Town Taxes 1/1/13 to 4/14/13	$365.04	14 City/Town Taxes 1/1/13 to 4/14/13	$365.04
13 County Taxes to		15 County Taxes to	
14 Assessments to		16 Assessments to	
15		17	
16		18	
17		19	
CALCULATION		**CALCULATION**	
Total Due from Borrower at Closing (K)	$189,762.30	Total Due to Seller at Closing (M)	$180,080.00
Total Paid Already by or on Behalf of Borrower at Closing (L)	– $175,615.04	Total Due from Seller at Closing (N)	– $115,665.04
Cash to Close ☒ From ☐ To Borrower	**$14,147.26**	**Cash ☐ From ☒ To Seller**	**$64,414.96**

Closing Disclosure - Bottom of Page 2

Additional Information About This Loan

Loan Disclosures

Assumption

If you sell or transfer this property to another person, your lender

☐ will allow, under certain conditions, this person to assume this loan on the original terms.

☒ will not allow assumption of this loan on the original terms.

Demand Feature

Your loan

☐ has a demand feature, which permits your lender to require early repayment of the loan. You should review your note for details.

☒ does not have a demand feature.

Late Payment

If your payment is more than *15* days late, your lender will charge a late fee of *5% of the monthly principal and interest payment.*

Negative Amortization (Increase in Loan Amount)

Under your loan terms, you

☐ are scheduled to make monthly payments that do not pay all of the interest due that month. As a result, your loan amount will increase (negatively amortize), and your loan amount will likely become larger than your original loan amount. Increases in your loan amount lower the equity you have in this property.

☐ may have monthly payments that do not pay all of the interest due that month. If you do, your loan amount will increase (negatively amortize), and, as a result, your loan amount may become larger than your original loan amount. Increases in your loan amount lower the equity you have in this property.

☒ do not have a negative amortization feature.

Escrow Account

For now, your loan

☒ will have an escrow account (also called an "impound" or "trust" account) to pay the property costs listed below. Without an escrow account, you would pay them directly, possibly in one or two large payments a year. Your lender may be liable for penalties and interest for failing to make a payment.

Escrow		
Escrowed Property Costs over Year 1	$2,473.56	Estimated total amount over year 1 for your escrowed property costs: *Homeowner's Insurance Property Taxes*
Non-Escrowed Property Costs over Year 1	$1,800.00	Estimated total amount over year 1 for your non-escrowed property costs: *Homeowner's Association Dues* You may have other property costs.
Initial Escrow Payment	$412.25	A cushion for the escrow account you pay at closing. See Section G on page 2.
Monthly Escrow Payment	$206.13	The amount included in your total monthly payment.

☐ will not have an escrow account because ☐ you declined it ☐ your lender does not offer one. You must directly pay your property costs, such as taxes and homeowner's insurance. Contact your lender to ask if your loan can have an escrow account.

Closing Disclosure – Top of Page 3

Partial Payments

Your lender

☒ may accept payments that are less than the full amount due (partial payments) and apply them to your loan.

☐ may hold them in a separate account until you pay the rest of the payment, and then apply the full payment to your loan.

☐ does not accept any partial payments.

If this loan is sold, your new lender may have a different policy.

Security Interest

You are granting a security interest in

456 Somewhere Ave., Anytown, ST 12345

You may lose this property if you do not make your payments or satisfy other obligations for this loan.

No Escrow		
Estimated Property Costs over Year 1		Estimated total amount over year 1. You must pay these costs directly, possibly in one or two large payments a year.
Escrow Waiver Fee		

In the future,

Your property costs may change and, as a result, your escrow payment may change. You may be able to cancel your escrow account, but if you do, you must pay your property costs directly. If you fail to pay your property taxes, your state or local government may (1) impose fines and penalties or (2) place a tax lien on this property. If you fail to pay any of your property costs, your lender may (1) add the amounts to your loan balance, (2) add an escrow account to your loan, or (3) require you to pay for property insurance that the lender buys on your behalf, which likely would cost more and provide fewer benefits than what you could buy on your own.

Closing Disclosure - Bottom of Page 3

Loan Calculations

Total of Payments. Total you will have paid after you make all payments of principal, interest, mortgage insurance, and loan costs, as scheduled. — $285,803.36

Finance Charge. The dollar amount the loan will cost you. — $118,830.27

Amount Financed. The loan amount available after paying your upfront finance charge. — $162,000.00

Annual Percentage Rate (APR). Your costs over the loan term expressed as a rate. This is not your interest rate. — 4.174%

Total Interest Percentage (TIP). The total amount of interest that you will pay over the loan term as a percentage of your loan amount. — 69.46%

Questions? If you have questions about the loan terms or costs on this form, use the contact information below. To get more information or make a complaint, contact the Consumer Financial Protection Bureau at **www.consumerfinance.gov/mortgage-closing**

Other Disclosures

Appraisal
If the property was appraised for your loan, your lender is required to give you a copy at no additional cost at least 3 days before closing. If you have not yet received it, please contact your lender at the information listed below.

Contract Details
See your note and security instrument for information about
 • what happens if you fail to make your payments,
 • what is a default on the loan,
 • situations in which your lender can require early repayment of the loan, and
 • the rules for making payments before they are due.

Liability after Foreclosure
If your lender forecloses on this property and the foreclosure does not cover the amount of unpaid balance on this loan,
☒ state law may protect you from liability for the unpaid balance. If you refinance or take on any additional debt on this property, you may lose this protection and have to pay any debt remaining even after foreclosure. You may want to consult a lawyer for more information.
☐ state law does not protect you from liability for the unpaid balance.

Refinance
Refinancing this loan will depend on your future financial situation, the property value, and market conditions. You may not be able to refinance this loan.

Tax Deductions
If you borrow more than this property is worth, the interest on the loan amount above this property's fair market value is not deductible from your federal income taxes. You should consult a tax advisor for more information.

Closing Disclosure - Top of Page 4

Contact Information

	Lender	Mortgage Broker	Real Estate Broker (B)	Real Estate Broker (S)	Settlement Agent
Name	Ficus Bank		Omega Real Estate Broker Inc.	Alpha Real Estate Broker Co.	Epsilon Title Co.
Address	4321 Random Blvd. Somecity, ST 12340		789 Local Lane Sometown, ST 12345	987 Suburb Ct. Someplace, ST 12340	123 Commerce Pl. Somecity, ST 12344
NMLS ID					
ST License ID			Z765416	Z61456	Z61616
Contact	Joe Smith		Samuel Green	Joseph Cain	Sarah Arnold
Contact NMLS ID	12345				
Contact ST License ID			P16415	P51461	PT1234
Email	joesmith@ ficusbank.com		sam@omegare.biz	joe@alphare.biz	sarah@ epsilontitle.com
Phone	123-456-7890		123-555-1717	321-555-7171	987-555-4321

Confirm Receipt

By signing, you are only confirming that you have received this form. You do not have to accept this loan because you have signed or received this form.

Applicant Signature	Date	Co-Applicant Signature	Date

Closing Disclosure - Bottom of Page 4

Closing Disclosure

This form is a statement of final loan terms and closing costs. Compare this document with your Loan Estimate.

Closing Information

Date Issued	4/15/2013
Closing Date	4/15/2013
Disbursement Date	4/15/2013
Settlement Agent	Epsilon Title Co.
File #	12-3456
Property	456 Somewhere Ave
	Anytown, ST 12345
Sale Price	$180,000

Transaction Information

Borrower	Michael Jones and Mary Stone
	123 Anywhere Street
	Anytown, ST 12345
Seller	Steve Cole and Amy Doe
	321 Somewhere Drive
	Anytown, ST 12345
Lender	Ficus Bank

Loan Information

Loan Term	30 years
Purpose	Purchase
Product	Fixed Rate
Loan Type	☒ Conventional ☐ FHA
	☐ VA ☐ _____
Loan ID #	123456789
MIC #	000654321

Loan Terms

Loan Terms		Can this amount increase after closing?
Loan Amount	$162,000	NO
Interest Rate	3.875%	NO
Monthly Principal & Interest *See Projected Payments below for your Estimated Total Monthly Payment*	$761.78	NO
		Does the loan have these features?
Prepayment Penalty	YES	• As high as $3,240 if you pay off the loan during the first 2 years
Balloon Payment	NO	

Closing Disclosure - Top of Page 5

Projected Payments

Payment Calculation	Years 1-7	Years 8-30
Principal & Interest	$761.78	$761.78
Mortgage Insurance	+ 82.35	+ —
Estimated Escrow *Amount can increase over time*	+ 206.13	+ 206.13
Estimated Total Monthly Payment	**$1,050.26**	**$967.91**

Estimated Taxes, Insurance & Assessments *Amount can increase over time* *See page 4 for details*	$356.13 a month	This estimate includes ☒ Property Taxes ☒ Homeowner's Insurance ☒ Other: Homeowner's Association Dues *See Escrow Account on page 4 for details. You must pay for other property costs separately.*	In escrow? YES YES NO

Costs at Closing

Closing Costs	$9,712.10	Includes $4,694.05 in Loan Costs + $5,018.05 in Other Costs – $0 in Lender Credits. *See page 2 for details.*
Cash to Close	$14,147.26	Includes Closing Costs. *See Calculating Cash to Close on page 3 for details.*

Closing Disclosure - Bottom of Page 5

At the Closing Table

You will be asked to sign a huge stack of papers at the closing table. The ones that you should pay close attention to are:

- Closing Disclosure – As discussed earlier, be sure the figures are accurate.
- Note – This is your promise to pay back the loan to the mortgage company. Be absolutely sure that the interest rate, term, etc., are correct.
- Deed of Trust –If you don't pay, you don't get to stay. This document describes how they will confiscate the house if you are delinquent.
- IRS Documents – On any IRS related document, be certain that your social security number is correct so that you can deduct the mortgage interest from your taxes.
- Make sure your Temporary Lease is in order.

All the rest of the documents are usually fluff. At closing, you'll receive copies of everything you signed, your survey, and home warranty information. Your agent will make arrangements to deliver your keys after funding.

Funding

Once both the buyer and the seller have signed the papers, the monies are wired from the lender to the title company. The title company then pays off the seller's mortgage (if they have one), the insurance companies, real estate agents, and any other party to the transaction that is entitled to receive payment. Once the transaction has funded, the house is officially yours! You can take possession according to the terms of any temporary lease agreed upon by you and the seller (discussed earlier).

Recording

The recording process is the final step in the closing process. The closing company, attorney, or title company that handles your transaction will complete the recording. The process officially records certain documents such as the warranty deed and the security instrument.

{ 11 }

After the Close

Do you think you're done after the papers are signed and you receive your keys? You're not.

Meeting Your New Financial Obligations

You should receive a payment coupon for your first house payment at closing. Do not be surprised if you receive a letter from the lender telling you that your loan has been sold. This is a very common practice. The lender will tell you where to mail your payments if your loan was sold, and you should receive a coupon booklet in the mail from the new lender, which is now your loan servicer. Even if you do not receive a payment coupon, you need to make your payments on time. Contact the loan servicer for payment information.

The loan servicer will keep track of your payment history and will apply your monthly loan payment to the balance and escrow reserves. The loan servicer is responsible for paying your real estate taxes and hazard insurance from the escrow reserves. While the tax and insurance bills should go directly to the loan servicer, they may come to you. If so, just forward them to the servicer for payment. Your payment may increase in the future if a higher escrow balance is needed to meet rising real estate tax or insurance costs. The loan servicer will provide a year-end interest statement and account analysis so that you can monitor this. You will also need this information when you file your taxes to ensure you take the appropriate deductions for the interest and real estate taxes you have paid. Consult your tax adviser with any questions.

Homestead Exemptions

A homestead exemption reduces the value of a home for state and local tax purposes. Once you file the appropriate paperwork with your local tax office, you are eligible for a sizable discount on your property taxes. Ask your Realtor for more information, or contact your local tax office for instructions on how to file.

Prepaying Your Mortgage

Prepaying part of your mortgage allows you to pay a lot less in interest. For every extra dollar you apply toward your loan principal, you save about two dollars in interest. For example, on a $200,000 loan with a five percent interest rate, paying an extra $50/month will save you almost $21,000 over the life of the loan, and the loan term will be reduced by almost three years. That means your 30-year loan becomes a 27-year loan. The same result can be obtained by making one extra mortgage payment a year. If you decide to prepay your mortgage, don't sign up for the "bi-weekly prepayment program" that your lender will offer you. These programs require that you pay a setup fee of about $300-400, plus a $5-8 per month service charge. You can almost always prepay at no charge. Just add the extra amount to your normal monthly payment, or pay the extra amount separately so it is easier to audit later.

Here Come The Scams!

When you buy a house, the deed is recorded with the county and becomes public record. Businesses create mailing lists of people who just bought a home and try to sell them things. The junk mail is endless! On the plus side, you do receive lots of valuable coupons to furniture stores, home improvement centers, and many other retail establishments, so keep your eyes open for those if you're a coupon cutter. But be on the lookout for the following scams:

Homestead Scams

Filing your homestead exemption is free. Scammers will send you very official looking documents with filing instructions and charge you $25-$50 to record the document for you. Don't fall for this one! Just go online to your county's appraisal district and look for filing instructions. Some counties even let you file your exemption online.

Mortgage Scams

We've already discussed the benefits of making biweekly mortgage payments or paying a little extra with your normal monthly payment. You don't have to pay your mortgage company or any other company to do this; you can make the extra payment at no charge any time. I recommend sending a separate check (or second online payment) and specify in the memo field that it be applied toward "principal only." Be on the lookout for companies that try to get you to send them your mortgage payment, claiming that they will make your payment for you. If you ever get a letter stating that your loan was sold or transferred to another bank and that you should start sending your payments to a different address, call the old bank and verify this information before you send any money.

Mortgage Insurance

After closing, you'll start receiving offers from numerous insurance companies. The policy they try to sell you is one that makes your house payment for you if you die or become disabled. You are generally better off buying a normal term life policy and/or disability insurance. Mortgage insurance policies are overpriced and sometimes underwritten by less than reputable insurance companies. What good is insurance if the company is bankrupt when you need it?

Predatory Refinancing

Refinancing your home can help reduce monthly payments and is a great financial planning tool when it is used responsibly and properly. It costs several thousand dollars to refinance your home, and those who make a habit of refinancing can very quickly end up owing far more than the house is worth.

When borrowers refinance their homes repeatedly to take out all of their equity, it is called equity stripping. While there are legitimate reasons to cash out the equity in your home, it is important for your financial future to build equity in your home.

Foreclosure "Rescue" Scams

If you are having problems making your mortgage payment, contact your lender as quickly as possible and see what options they offer. Definitely avoid any business that:

- Provide a money back guarantee that says they can stop the foreclosure
- Advises you not to contact your lender
- Tries to collect a fee from you

- Only accepts a cashier's check or wire transfer
- Advises you to make your mortgage payment directly to them
- Tries to get you to transfer your title

Contracts for Deed

A contract for deed is often called "rent-to-own" financing and is commonly used with seller-financed transactions. Under a contract for deed, the property title remains in the name of the seller until the buyer has made a certain number of payments and sometimes until after he or she has paid off the house completely. Although the seller is supposed to transfer the title to the buyer after they have paid off the house, this doesn't always happen. Basically, the buyers are paying for a house that they very often will never really own. Contracts for deed are a great deal for the seller, but are a nightmare for the buyer.

Rent-to-Own

Not a day goes by that I don't answer a question about rent-to-own transactions. They work like this: If a buyer can't qualify for a traditional mortgage, a seller might agree to rent them the house for a period of time while the buyer gets his or her finances in order. At the end of the lease term, they buy the house through traditional financing, at a predetermined price (top dollar). The buyer typically pays a large option fee upfront, and a portion of the monthly rent is applied toward the sales price of the home.

In theory, it sounds great. More often than not, however, the buyer doesn't qualify for their loan, and they lose their option fee and all their potential equity in the house. *Rent-to-own is a great deal for the seller, but a horrible, horrible plan for the buyer.*

Renting and buying should be treated as two separate transactions, not rolled into one. If you can't qualify for a traditional mortgage, rent until you can.

If you insist on renting to own, hire a lawyer and not a Realtor. Most of us are not qualified to protect you in these transactions.

Rental Scams

Scammers have been hijacking rental ads by changing the contact information and reposting the modified ad on another site. Or, they make up rentals that don't exist. The goal is to get you to pay a security deposit or first month's rent before you find out it's a scam. Beware of anyone who tells you to wire money or if they want a security deposit or first month's rent before you've met or signed a lease. Try to confirm the identity of the agent showing you the home.

Reverse Mortgages

Reserve mortgages allow homeowners 62 years or older to borrow against the equity in their home and not repay it until after they move out or die. But scammers have come up with about 5 or 6 different ways to steal the equity in the homes of unsuspecting seniors. With promises of free loans that can be used to finance expensive vacations and other luxuries, some lenders are aggressively pitching loans to homeowners who cannot afford the fees or even the property taxes and maintenance on their home. Reverse mortgages can be a valuable tool for seniors to stay in their homes and access their equity, but getting involved with the wrong lender is a recipe for disaster. If you're in the market for a reverse mortgage, be on the lookout for high pressure sales tactics, tricky advertising, understating the risk of losing the home, and being asked to leave your spouse off your loan.

{ 12 }

What Can Go Wrong

In homebuying, much can go wrong. Besides your Realtor, at least 15-20 other professionals are involved in a real estate transaction, and while they all have the same goal in mind, things happen that delay closing or forfeit the sale. Here are some examples:

- The survey shows an encroachment or other problem
- The lender cannot clear the borrower's loan conditions in time
- The buyer creates a problem with his credit by opening new lines of credit or switching jobs
- Hail, wind, fire, vandals, etc., damage the property
- The title search finds a lien against the property, and the seller does not have the cash to clear it
- During the final walk through, new damage or theft is discovered, or the seller removed things from the home that were supposed to stay
- The title company does not receive documents in time for closing
- Seller changes their mind or refuses to move

- Seller is buying a new home and there is a problem with that transaction
- Seller dies
- There is a hailstorm between inspection and closing, and the roof needs to be re-inspected
- Buyer loses their job so their loan is denied

Some things are just beyond anyone's control, so there is no point in worrying about the improbable things that can go wrong. Resolving these issues takes a great deal of communication, some compromise, and levelheaded real estate professionals on both sides. Do your part, and more than likely everything will work out in the end.

Final Thoughts

There you have it! What you need to know about buying a home. Yes, it is complicated and sometimes stressful, but it is worth the time you invested in reading this book to educate and protect yourself.

Start by hiring a great agent to represent you, and do not ever sign anything until you have a thorough understanding of your risks, responsibilities, and your rights. Don't be a lazy buyer!

Most of all, know that before long you will be moving into your new home, and the stress of the homebuying process will be long forgotten. You will be putting down roots and becoming part of a new community. Many, many firsts will take place in your new home, and countless memories will be created.

My hope is that I have been able to help you avoid the horrible, gut-wrenching, stress-inducing process that buying a home can be, and that you will have many years of happiness in your new home. Feel free to contact me at Alysse@HelpUBuyAmerica if you have questions about the process, or if you need a referral to an EBA in your area. If you are buying a home in Dallas, Houston, or Austin, we'd love to assist you. Happy House Hunting!

ABOUT THE AUTHOR

Alysse Musgrave is the broker/owner of HelpUBuy America and a graduate of Texas A&M University and the Sheffield School of Interior Design. She is a contributing writer for Zillow Group and the author of 4 books including the highly acclaimed and best-selling "Buying a Home: Don't Let Them Make a Monkey Out of You!" HelpUBuy America is an Exclusive Buyer Agency whose mission it is to protect the rights of homebuyers in Austin, Houston, and Dallas.